PIONEER PREACHER IN IDAHO

Kamiah-Grangeville Country

PIONEER PREACHER

IN

IDAHO

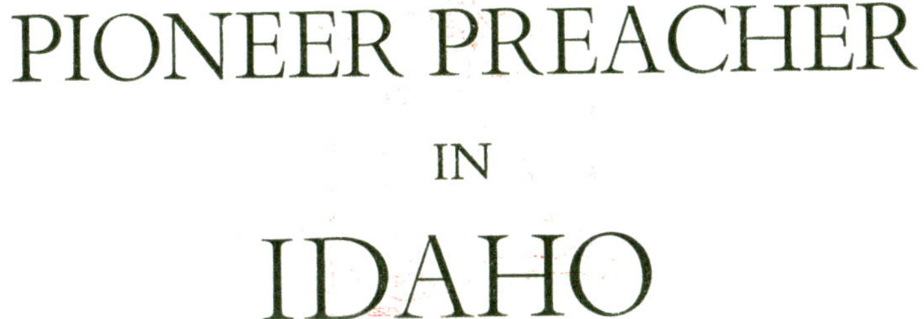

JAMES A. HEDGES

YE GALLEON PRESS

FAIRFIELD, WASHINGTON

1981

Library of Congress Cataloging in Publication Data

Hedges, James A.
    Pioneer preacher in Idaho.

    Reprinted from Journal of the Presbyterian Historical Society, Sept.
1949, and two succeeding issues.
    Includes index.
    1. Hedges, James A. 2. Presbyterian Church—Clergy—Biography.
3. Clergy--Idaho--Biography.   4. Pioneers—Idaho—Biography.   5.
Idaho—Biography.
    I. Title.
BX9225.H353A33   285'.13[B]   81-11597
ISBN 0-87770-249-7   AACR2

INTRODUCTION

Idaho! The very last of the fifty states which make up our republic to be visited by white men (Lewis and Clark party in 1805) remained pioneer country a bit longer than much of the surrounding territory.

This pioneer life with its adventures, customs, and thrills has been expertly caught and related by the Rev. James A. Hedges during his forty years in the state. He came to Idaho during the time when the memories of its first settlers were still vivid and, in fact, many of the pioneers were still living and became known to Hedges.

His experience was anything but sheltered and a few of his adventures include: a flood, a fire raging through a town, a runaway train, and his attendance at a wild Indian dance which Christians had been forbidden to attend, the suicide of a young girl in her wedding dress, having his horse die in the middle of the road and other such events. Hedges relates each experience with a touch of humor, concern or thrill depending on the occasion. His stories are of such a nature that they would add spice to anyone's conversation. And many of his adventures would make excellent conversation pieces.

The Rev. James A. Hedges, after having obtained two degrees from Wittenberg College, enrolled in McCormick Theological Seminary in Chicago. Following his graduation and ordination he went to White Sulphur Springs, Montana, where he served a church there for three or four years. Then he accepted a call to become a home missionary in Idaho. He left his wife and baby in Montana while he sought a place to live. He could find nothing suitable and rented a cottage in Lewisotn and went back to visit his family as often as he could.

He tells of his adventures in that part of Idaho through which Lewis and Clark had journeyed and near where the Reverend and Mrs. Henry Harmon Spalding had established their mission home. He came to know the workers at the McBeth Mission and others. He describes the geography of the area, and relates what happened to him, relating it in the most readable and charming fashion.

His story reveals the beauty he sees in the countryside, the character and personalities of the residents, both Indian and white; the conflicts, the difficulties, the disappointrnents and the joys; his own and the people he writes about. His is a vivid description of the river at flood stage with its distructiveness, the terror when a fire sweeps through the town, the runaway train which resulted in a terrible crash near the town—all make for good reading. He relates a story of his visit to the McBeth Mission to the Nez Perce Indians and the influence it had on the tribe. He adds to our understanding of the early Nez Perce ministers trained by the McBeths and their part in the life of the church and the changes which they help make in the tribal life.

During his forty years in Idaho he served the church in both the northern and southern part of the state. He began his work in the Camas Prairie and Clearwater River country, which was the traditional home of the Nez Perce Indians. He was not, however, a missionary to the Indians but rather served in establishing churches in the frontier towns of Nezperce, Juliaetta and Kendrick. He had to travel by stagecoach and on one occasion it was necessary for him to take over the reins of the driver, he had to cross the rivers by ferry, drive his own wagon or carriage over roads that were mere trails that the Indians had used to travel on horseback.

He closed his ministry in Idaho at Pocatello in southern Idaho which enabled him to privide historical reminiscences from much of that state and thus add to one's knowledge of early life in that area.

Readers of this little book should look forward as they turn its pages to being entertained with its humor, thrilled by its adventures, moved by its discouragement and tragedies, and being informed by its descriptions of territory, people and events. A small book — that should not be filed away on a shelf but rather kept handy to pick up and reread passages which speak to one's mood at the time.

E. Paul Hovey
Portland, Oregon

Former Moderator, Synod of Idaho
Former Minister, The Congregational
Presbyterian (Federated) Church,
Lewiston, Idaho.
Member, The Spalding Museum Foundation

JOURNAL

OF

The Presbyterian Historical Society

Vol. XXVII   SEPTEMBER, 1949   No. 3

PIONEER PREACHER IN IDAHO

BY JAMES A. HEDGES

[This is the eye-witness story of a pioneer Presbyterian missionary who, as a young man fresh from theological seminary, packed his bag in Chicago and ventured into the Rocky mountains. In Idaho he found primitive human conditions amid scenic grandeur. This is a story of human struggle, eager, courageous, dramatic. High obstacles raised themselves against this champion of spiritual ideals. The success or failure of mission work in the mountains depended on the quality and ability of the man in the field, and on the wisdom of the Board back east. In the midst of the battle for righteousness the writer makes an appraisal of the strategy pursued by the Church. And he gives some vivid pictures of Indians and whites. For forty years beginning before the turn of the last century (1894) this missionary labored under conditions of constant hardship. He reveals the devotion of the missionaries of the Cross.

Rev. James A. Hedges was a graduate of Wittenberg College at which he also earned the degree of Master of Arts. After completing his theological course at McCormick Seminary in 1894, he was ordained by Great Falls Presbytery and served the Presbyterian Church at White Sulphur Springs, Montana, for four years. Then he went to Idaho as a home missionary, and it is at this point that the following narrative begins. He continued his missionary work in the west until his retirement in 1936. The complete manuscript is in the archives of the Presbyterian Historical Society.—THE EDITORS.]

The next morning I took the train for Juliaetta, Idaho, the then terminus of the Palouse Branch of the Northern Pacific railway system. As I rode down through the beautiful rolling hills of the Palouse country, I was more and more convinced that I had reached the land of my dreams. They were covered to their summits with wheat just beginning to ripen and I thought I had never seen a more beautiful country. After the Palouse hills we began to go down the long Potlatch Canyon that I was to come to know so well, whose walls at frequent intervals were formed of long prismatic columns of basalt and whose slopes were covered with pines and shrubs and wild flowers and green grasses. We rode down this for a half hour or more. I was more and more charmed by the richness of the scenery and the little farms that lay on the benches of the canyon. Orchards and fields and vineyards of hardy pioneers whom we come to know in after years. Down through the canyon from the very beginning flowed the waters of Little Bear joining the Big Bear both emptying farther down into the Potlatch. I grow homesick as I write of them. We passed through the little town of Kendrick which afterward was to be our home for seven year[s] but then had no interest for me.

Crossing Potlatch Canyon

We reached Juliaetta after dark. It gained its name from the names of the two daughters of the man who laid it out. One was called Julia and the other Etta. He combined the two names giving it the unique and very feminine name of Juliaetta. He was also the hotel keeper with a patriarchal and benevolent countenance. From there we were to take the stage the next morning for Nezperce, seventy five miles away. I was up bright and early and took a good look at the little town lying on the northern slope of the Potlatch Canyon and very picturesque. Its homes and fields and orchards looked as though they would slide off into the river while above them the canyon sloped upward for several miles. The canyon on the other side looked much steeper. The road we were to take ran up it in a series of switchbacks. After breakfast we started on our long ride to Nezperce. There were several passengers beside myself some of them women. The driver was an inexperienced young fellow who knew little about horses. The stage was an open one. Slowly we climbed up the long winding grade in the broiling sun, stopping frequently to let the horses blow. It gave us opportunity also to look far up and down the canyon which was very beautiful at that time of the year.

A Feast for Eye and Soul

On we climbed untill we came out on top of a beautiful rolling prairie called the Potlatch Ridge. Here were farm homes that showed evidence of comfort and prosperity. For eight or ten miles we drove across this rich looking rolling prairie which lay two thousand feet above our starting point of the morning down there at the bottom of the Potlatch Canyon. The whole region was an elevated plateau some three thousand feet above sea level and broken into sections called Ridges by the two thousand feet deep canyons of the Potlatch and Clearwater Rivers, with their several tributaries. For a hundred miles it stretched from the Bitter Root range of the Rockies on the north and east to Craig's Mountain—which was not really a mountain but another high plateau—south and west of the Clearwater River. What a feast for eye and soul. I have seen no fairer region anywhere.

* The captions in boldface type have been supplied by the Editors.

In the afternoon we came to the breaks of the Clearwater. As we made our way slowly down the rough winding grade, we got glimpses, both up and down, and for miles and miles, of the beautiful river. It was some two thousand feet below us and flowed like a silver thread through its canyon whose rugged sides were hidden by green pines and shrubbery and grass and ferns. How I feasted my eyes on this panorama of forest and stream, of rugged hills and sunlit valley. It helped me to forget the physical torture down over stony and bumpy road.

We arrived at the stage station on the banks of the river about five o'clock in the evening, and here we had to stay all night. The station was a good sized frame shack. Inside, on the first floor, was a sort of rude office where was kept a bucket of water and tin basin which was provided for the guests to wash off the dust and stain of travel and wipe them on a towel that was black with the dirt and dust of other travelers. There was a fair sized dining room and the supper that evening was thick beefsteak, fried potatoes, gravy and fried eggs, and black coffee. There was also cornbread and hot biscuits. For dessert we had prunes. At bed time we were taken up stairs where there was just one large room. Thin curtains divided the beds of the women from those of the men. If the women used a candle all their doings and undoings could be plainly seen.

Ferrying Across the Clearwater River

In the morning, after a breakfast of ham and eggs and hot cakes and coffee, we climbed aboard the somewhat rickety stage and started for Nezperce still fifty miles away. We were ferried across the river by the usual ferry of those days. The ferry was a flat bottomed barge about twenty five feet long and twelve feet wide. It had a railing on each side and gates at each end, with hinged platforms at the back and front to enable stock and passengers to enter and leave the ferry when these were let down and rested on the bank. A long cable was stretched from shore to shore between high poles, and another cable was fastened to a grooved pulley which ran along the main cable. Cables from the two ends of the ferry boat was [sic.] fastened to this second cable by means of hooks. The current sweeping against the side of the boat caused it to be carried across the stream by means of the pulley running along the main cable.

We were carried across in about fifteen minutes and then commenced the long climb upward out of the canyon, over a winding grade that ran through scattered pines and past the new shacks of the settlers, for we were now on the newly opened reservation. It was a beautiful morning in june and the ferns and wild roses, and the yellow and purple of other flowers mingled well with the green grass and scattered pines and firs and the brown plowed fields where growing crops were just beginning to be seen. Up and up we climbed for this was the slope of Craig's Mountain. Farther and farther untill our vision took in the hills around Lewiston twenty five miles away we ascended. Back of us were the fields and orchards of the Potlatch of yesterday. Ahead of us was the tree lined edge of Craig's Mountain over which we were to pass. Below us we had glimpses of the Clearwater flowing along in its beautiful setting of rugged hills.

About eleven o'clock we came out on top of Craig's Mountain up whose sides we had been climbing. And there stretching away before us, on gently rolling hills, was a great forest of pine, fir, and spruce, without underbrush and looking like a well kept park. The road wound in and out and under great trees, in gentle grades for the most of the way of ten miles through the forest untill we came to a place called Kippen or Cold Springs which was the stopping place for dinner. It stood beside a little stream which had its source in some springs a little distance away. I was often to stop here in months to come. It was kept by a man by the name of Kippen who several months later was shot and killed by a neighboring settler whom he accused of being on too intimate terms with his wife. I was at the trial in Lewiston of the man and the woman. He was a well known civil engineer. Both were acquitted.

To get back to our story, we had dinner and then set out for Nezperce still twenty miles away. We soon came out on a great prairie of rolling hills. It was covered with the most luxuriant grass sprinkled with flowers of many colors. There it stretched away before us without a tree or bush to be seen, just a rolling meadow crossed here and there by Indian trails worn deep by centuries of travel by the Nez Perces. There was hardly a fence to be seen as the settlers had not yet begun to fence their claims.

Handling a Balky Team

It rained on us shortly afre [after] we left the timber and the road became heavy and sticky. Our team was a balky one though the fault was mostly with the driver. It was also very slight and we had to pile out of the stage at every little hill for they were not able to pull up those sticky muddy roads. This became monotonous to us in a little while and was especially hard on the women. Finally at the solicitations of the other passengers I took the lines from the hands of the inexperienced driver. From that on we had no difficulty with the balky team. Nor did we have to get out and walk as formerly. The team proved amply strong enough to pull us up hill and down hill and showed no sign of wanting to balk. It was not that I was an expert in handling horses but because the driver was utterly ignorant.

As we topped the last hill and got our first glimpse of the little new town, only a few months old, sprawling there on a naked and ugly flat between two ranges of low hills, my heart almost stopped its beating. I thought of the wife and baby back there in Montana. That place seemed like everything worth while in comparison to this. I thought of the long rough stage ride from Juliaetta to this place and wondered how I could ever bring them to this place.

It lay, a little cluster of rough unpainted shacks and store buildings without the sign of a tree, in a dreary hollow between two ranges of low hills. The nearer we got to it the drearier it seemed. But I had come on the mission of Him who said "Go ye into all the world" and I meant to do it here also. As I rode over that magnificent prairie that afternoon and saw how it was filling up with settlers, I said "Here is a great future. Here is a great field. I will give my life to it. What a heritage of faith it ought to become." But it was not to be.

After delivering the mail to the little postoffice and depositing the other passengers into waiting wagons that were there to receive them, I was driven to the "Hotel." I soon discovered that all other hotels I had known no matter how stingy and uncouth they might be, were palatial beside this. Made of rough boards, two stories in height, it was set down in the midst of a muddy and dreary lot, without a walk into it save the muddy earth. Indians and half breeds were stalking about in dirty blankets and altogether it was the most unprepossessing looking inn I had ever seen. And the interior gave no promise of anything better. I went in to the little dirty office where on a dingy and dirty desk lay the register. Gingerly I took up the pen to write my name. There was mud all over the floor. An old chair held a tin wash basin and a tin bucket of water sat on an upturned box. This was the lavatory where saint and sinner, Indian and white man, washed their faces in the tin basin and wiped them on a common dirty and greasy towel.

A Hotel to Remember

The landlord was a Scotchman, a loyal Presbyterian but no Christian. He was a whisky guzzler, a horse thief, with an old and honorable name, and married to an Indian woman who was far better than he. He came in and took my grips and led me upstairs to my room. At first he was surly and evil looking. After finding who I was he became most respectful in his speech and behavior though it was clearly to be seen he was cannily watching me out of the corner of his eye. I had never occupied a bed or a room like that before. The room was barren of furniture except a chair and bed; nails were driven into the rough board partition to hang one's clothes on; the floor was as barren as when it was laid and splintery; the bed was a cheap iron affair on which was a greasy mattress and filthy bed clothes and on which some wild man, Indian or white, had slept the night before. All of these things made me think of the inner prison in which two ancient pilgrims were thrust at Philippi. I found it impossible to sing songs as did they. God shut the mouths of lions for Daniel but left the creeping things for me. I am sure that Daniel had a better night's rest than I.

And the supper and the breakfast that followed! Would that I could forget them. The only other gastronomical experience that I remember as being worse than this was a Chinese dinner in a famous Chinese restaurant in the city of San Francisco in Chinatown. I would rather feast on bread and water than to endure the sight and taste again of famous Chinese cooking in the famous Chinese quarters of a famous American city, or of the lesser known but of no less unsavory concoctions of an Indian woman on a very famous Indian reservation. It was with a very thankful heart that I walked out the next morning to get acquainted with the little town and to find out what Christian and Presbyterian folks were therein. I was not afraid to face any of the latter I might find after my night's experience at McCleod's Hotel.

I soon found one or two and they were about as good representatives of the Kirk as McCleod. One was a merchant, having a very considerable stock of general merchandise, a Hoosier by birth, a Presbyterian by training, and a periodic drinker by choice. It is only fair to say that this was about his only vice. He tried manfully to overcome it and great was his disgust and remorse when he would break over and go on a spree. He hadn't yet learned the secret of victory. He loved music and was a fair pipe organist. He always played the organ for church services and played it well even if he was not quite sober. The other Presbyterian I found that morning was a Kentuckian, a blue grasser, with all the Kentuckian's reverence for a woman and a horse. He was always coldly sober and steady going. He had a blooded saddle horse which he rode every day and he was very proud of him. He did the butchering for the town and community. In his business dealings he was regarded as a bit twisty. There will be more of him as this story gets along. He had a wife, high strung and spirited, a Kentucky thoroughbred, and the mainstay of the little church. It has just been organized a few weeks.

I found a few other Christians but not many and none of them were good advertisements of their faith. The merchant invited me home for dinner and there I found a real if tiny home. There was a frame cottage painted white on the outside and clean and wholesome on the inside. I gave a great sigh of contentment as I found this oasis in that desert of hard conditions and hard living. The mistress of that house was a cultivated and refined woman, keeping her home as any cultured woman would do and the more noticeable in such surroundings. I was invited to make that my home for awhile and oh, the luxury of a clean room, a clean bed, and clean surroundings. So the Lord raises up for his servants houses and brethren and lands with persecutions. It was Friday night when I reached that little frontier settlement five days since I left the wife and baby in Montana.

The Hazardous Trail of the Missionary

Sunday morning I went down to the vacant store building where I was told that services were held whenever there was a service and that was only when the Sunday School Missionary passed through on his wide extended trips.

With his two wheeled cart, loaded down with Bibles and literature and drawn by his little gray cayuse, he was the great religious pioneer. Sabbath School missions was the greatest investment the church ever made. Nearly all of the great churches of the far west as well as the lesser were once only outposts on the hazardous trail of the Sunday School Missionary. And the names of the most of them are unknown to the church. But their monument is greater than human hands could ever build.

When I entered the door of that vacant store building that morning I found straw and paper and litter of every kind scattered over the floor; the wooden benches were all piled up in a corner or moved here and there in confusion of arrangement. Candle grease was on the floor and benches as there had been a band practice the night before and the only light they had was that of candles. I found a broom and went to work to sweep the floor and adjust the benches for service. I found an old shoe box and stood it on end for a pulpit. I dusted the benches and organ and sat down to wait for some to come in.

About half past nine they commenced to come and kept coming untill there was perhaps fifty people present for Sunday School. There being no superintendent I took charge and things began to adjust themselves. Several classes were formed and teachers chosen for that day at least and altogether I felt we were making a good beginning. When the Sunday School hour was over the most of the scholars and adults staid for church. By this time others had come in untill the room was practically filled. The merchant, of whom we have spoken, took his place at the organ and the instrumental music that day in that dingy old store room was as good as that heard in many cathedrals. The singing on the other hand was very primitive on the key and off the key, shrill and unmusical with a general result of the lack of all harmony. But the spirit was good. I do not know what I preached about that day but I felt I had real needy and hungry folks before me. In all I felt the service was good. In the evening we had another good service by candle light for as yet there were no lamps. And that was the only service for white people that day for twenty miles around.

The week following was spent in getting acquainted and getting settled. I found a room in a vacant store building opposite the store of the merchant in whose home I was entertained for a few days. Having furnished it with a new bed and mattress and chairs and a grass rug and other articles of furniture all bought of the same merchant, I moved in. I had brought a lot of bedding with me in my trunk and everything was scrupulously clean. There was another small room which I could use as a kitchen and in this I installed a small wood burning cook stove. When I asked where I could get fuel I was told to just go out and help myself to fence posts around some vacant lots whose owners had merely fenced them and gone away and left them. However I found a more honest way of getting wood than that by paying some one to bring it from Lawyer's Canyon some ten miles away.

13

An Indian Camp Meeting

I had not been there a week before I received a letter from one of the most famous missionaries to the Indians in the United States. It was from Miss Kate McBeth from her mission house at Lapwai, inviting me to come to Lapwai for a great campmeeting of the Nez Perce Christian Indians. It was the first they had ever held for reasons which will appear as my story goes on. It was to be held the last days of June and up untill the Fourth of July. I wrote her I would gladly come. Lapwai was sixty miles away down the slopes of Craig's Mountain and I did not know how I would get there as I had neither horse nor conveyance of any kind which was the only way of getting to and fro from the distant points of the reservation at that time. But I trusted that a way would be found. Let me say in passing, that the state of Idaho, at the time of my writing of this, is celebrating the one hundreth anniversary at Lapwai of the founding of the mission by Henry Spalding and his wife Eliza among the Nez Perce Indians. And the Presbyterian Church has made this whole year a centennial for the observance and celebration of the foundation work of Whitman and Spalding among the Cayuse and Nez Perce Indians. But more of this.

Along about the first of July I learned that one of the merchants of the town with another business man was going to drive to Lewiston, the county seat, some seventy five miles away, and they would necessarily pass through Lapwai in going and coming. This merchant was also a Presbyterian by upbringing and could recite the whole of the shorter catechism. But I have never heard a more profane man. I asked him if I might ride to Lapwai with him and he laughingly told me I could if I would take the consequences. It was a terrifically hot day and the spring wagon or hack as they called it had no top. Also there was only one seat which was occupied by the merchant and the other man. I sat on a box in the rear and sometimes I had hard work to stay in the vehicle at all because of the rough roads. The men took no pains to conceal that my presence was not welcome.

I will not soon forget that ride over the rolling prairie and through the timber on Craigs Mountain and down its northern slope into the canyon of the Lapwai flowing between lines of cottonwoods, through a green valley a mile or two in width. Rugged and barren hills except for the bunch grass that grew on them rose from a thousand to two thousand feet on either side. There were Indian teepees scattered all along the way. The farther down into the canyon the hotter it became and I never was so glad as when we stopped for dinner at Holt's Ranch, a white man who had married an Indian woman. It was a noted stopping place in those days having abundant shade and water and plenty of wholesome food. It was also the scene of many a mountain gathering.

After dinner we pushed on down the canyon, the stream winding its way through patches of alfalfa and grain and lines of cottonwood trees. More and more teepees appeared as we came down but we saw few Indians. They were in the great camps below. About the middle of the afternoon we came in sight of old Fort Lapwai, once a government post in the 60's and 70's but now transformed into a government school for Nez Perce boys and girls. On the other side of the road from the fort was a beautiful little meadow belonging to the government through which the Lapwai murmured on its way to the Clearwater. The commandant and superintendent of the school, Major McConnell, was an officer of the regular army and an elder of the Presbyterian church at Lewiston. He was afterward killed in the Spanish American War.

Meeting a Famous Missionary

On the banks of the Lapwai we saw a large circle of teepees with a large tent of meeting in the center which the men with whom I was riding told me gruffly was the Christian camp. We drove along a little farther and soon came to the Mission House itself for which I had been looking for many a weary hour. Its grounds bordered on the meadow in which was the Christian camp. Will I ever forget the warm welcome given me by that wonderful Christian woman whose work will never die. She was a plain Scotch body short of stature with kindly grey eyes that could grow very stern on occasion. She had a strong chin which showed a resolute will inflexible as adamant when a question of right arose. Yet she was one of the gentlest and sweetest of Christians.

How deliciously cool seemed the large study room and reception hall of the Mission House after my long hot ride sitting on a box in an open hack through sixty miles of the roughest road even though it passed through enchanting scenery. I was taken up stairs to the guest room, plain, comfortable, and cool, that seemed like a palace after my experience in Nezperce. Here I had a bath and general clean up and went down to visit with Miss McBeth and watch with great interest the things that were going on about me. On the other side of the Mission House from the Christian camp and about a half of mile down the stream was another very large circle of tepees where I could see blanketed Indians riding back and forth on their horses both men and beasts decorated in a barbarous and picturesque manner. I could hear a great drum beating continually "tum tum," "tum tum," "tum tum." Miss McBeth told me that this was the camp of a thousand wild Indians made up largely of Nez Perces but with a numerous sprinkling of many other tribes of the northwest.

From the days when the Hudson Bay Company occupied this whole region when their trappers and voyageurs trapped and hunted and sang up and down the streams and traded with the Indians, it had been the custom of these Indians to gather together about the first of July for a week or ten days or a month of riotous gambling and horse racing and trading of wives and nameless other debaucheries. It had been the custom of the Christian Indians from the days when Spalding established the mission to go into camp with the wild fellows.

Many of them went back to their old heathenism or were greatly hurt morally and spiritually by the unrestrained debauchery of the heathen camp. At the meeting of the Presbytery of Walla Walla that spring it had been resolved to establish a separate camp for the Christian Indians and while the heathen were engaging in all kinds of godless revelry to hold religious services under the leadership of the Indian ministers who had been trained in the mission schools of the McBeth sisters. Also white ministers of the presbytery.

It was all tremendously interesting to me. That afternoon after my bath and change of clothes I sat on the porch of the Mission House and watched the Christian Indians coming in their hacks or riding horseback from far distant Kamiah and Meadow Creek and North Fork and the nearer Lapwai. As one after another turned into the meadow where was the Christian camp I could hear the fervent "Thank God" of Miss McBeth. Or if some went on by to the heathen camp unable yet to resist its attractions I can hear her softly spoken word of sorrow that these were yet too weak to separate from that old camp where still were many of their relatives and friends in all the picturesque dress and deviltry of the heathen.

Never could I forget the first service I attended that evening in the tent of meeting in the Christian camp. Miss McBeth introduced me to the Indian ministers and people. How respectful and reverent. How clean and tidy in their dress. How dignifiedly they assembled for worship, the men sitting on one side and the women on the other. And how they sang. I sat there and wept for joy as they sang the old hymns that the Spaldings and the McBeth sisters had translated into their language. There were some of the newer gospel hymns also. For the first time I came to realize what Jesus Christ can do for an out and out heathen soul. For the first time I heard singing that burst from the surcharged hearts of men born out of savagery. Never will I hear its like untill I hear the redeemed singing in the meadow lands of heaven under the trees that grow by the river of the water of life.

An Eloquent Indian

Then came a sermon by Silas Whitman. I couldn't understand a word he said, but the eloquence of those speaking gestures, the smoothly flowing tongue, and the rapt spirit of the preacher was interpreted to my soul. I went away with Miss McBeth and Father Adair, of whom I shall speak again to the Mission House feeling lifted to the sevent[h] heaven by what I had seen and heard. That night after worship in the study room of the mission and Mr. Adair and I had retired to the upper room, I lay on my bed with one window open towards the Christian camp, and the other towards the heathen. I could hear the Christians holding their family worship in their teepees and from the other window the sullen beat of the "Tum, tum, Tum tum, Tum tum" as that great camp kept up its revelry and dancing and nameless wickedness all the night long.

The next day I saw as brave a thing as will be seen anywhere among any people. The great heathen camp had not taken kindly to the separation of the Christian camp from it. As is usual when men are called out of the world to follow the Lord Jesus Christ friends and companions resent it. They will not come themselves but they are furious when others separate themselves from them to serve the Lord.

A young minister by the name of Sibbetts and pastor of the Lewiston church had come out that morning to attend the campmeeting and was also staying at the Mission House. He and I were standing out in the yard in front of the house just inside the fence that separated the mission grounds from the road which led through the village of Lapwai past the great heathen camp and on into Lewiston twelve miles away. There was also a fence running at right angles to this separating the mission house and grounds from the meadow in which was the camp of the Christian Indians. A gate at the corner of the mission yard and meadow opened from the road in front into the meadow. It stood always open for anyone to go in and out as they pleased especially the Christian Indians. The road in front was the great thoroughfare over which settlers by the hundreds had poured and were pouring into the newly opened reservation for a hundred miles beyond. Long trains of freight wagons were passing by continually carrying freight to that upper country.

A Dangerous Encounter

Mr. Sibbetts and I were standing out there in the mission yard early in the morning watching with intense interest the whole picturesque and wonderful drama. The Almighty was doing great things and we were beholding his passing by. We heard a noise down the road toward the heathen camp and looking that way we saw a great crowd of wild fellows coming out of that camp having on their war paint and bonnets, riding on spirited horses and coming down the road toward us bent on riding into the Christian camp and breaking it up. They were led by Jim Reubens, head chief of the tribe and one of the wickedest of Indians. On they came chanting their "hi yi, ki yi, hi yi" on savage business bent. It was a stern and determined procession with their faces grim and set.

When Miss McBeth, who had come out to see what all the noise was about saw them coming she fled into the mission house to pray. Mr. Sibbetts and I stood there as if paralyzed watching the oncoming savages. We were afraid to stay and ashamed to run. Just then we saw five men riding out of the Christian camp with their horses at full gallop. They swept through the meadow gate on to the great road down which the savages were riding. They ranged themselves across it and remained seated like statues on their horses watching the approach of that savage procession. When the front line of the horde headed by Chief Reubens was perhaps within fifty feet of that line of horsemen stretched across the roadway, one of them, Edward Reboin, suddenly flung out his arm toward them and bade them halt. Chief Reubens his bonnet of eagle feathers sweeping the ground, threw up his hands and gave a sharp command to his savage followers and all stood in dignified silence for a few moments watching each other with keen eyes.

Then Edward Reboin and Chief Reubens for many minutes in speech after speech held council while all the rest kept silence. Finally a compromise was arranged to the effect that there should be a certain line established between the two camps beyond which none of either camp was to go as long as both camps remained in existence. Then at a signal from Reubens the wild horde which had come out to destroy and perhaps to kill wheeled and rode back to their camp in sullen dignity but they kept the truce. From that time there was no disturbance of the Christian camp nor did the Christian Indians go into the heathen camp. Wherein was the power of those five unarmed men facing a couple of hundred of armed savages bent on mischief? They had no weapons and were so few. The prayers of that grayed haired mission teacher were answered. Angels no doubt with flaming swords stood beside these men as once one stood in the way of Balaam of old. God's people can not be touched in the way of duty unless he wills it so.

On Forbidden Ground

On that same day I was guilty of a great breach of trust though I knew it not at the time. I have spoken of Mr. Adair. He was the titular head of the whole Nez Perce mission at the time. His name was Alexander Adair. He had been appointed head of the mission because the powers that be thought it sounded better and would have a better effect on the Indians to have a man at the head than a woman. But Miss McBeth was always the real head. That afternoon Mr. Adair and myself stood watching a great stir in the heathen camp down the creek. We saw a great band of naked savages come sweeping down the hillsides above the camp, yelling like demons and brandishing their fire arms and spears; behind them came women riding astride their ponies and adding their shrill cries to the yells of the warriors in front. We were told that the wild camp was staging a sham attack on an ene[my] village. Miss McBeth handed us her field glasses that we might see it the better laughing somewhat guiltily as she did so.

So much more interesting did the field glasses make the scene down there that I said to Mr. Adair "I would like to see that closer." And Mr. Adair said "I would too." And before Miss McBeth had time to stop us—she had gone into the house for a moment—away we went and we were half way to the heathen camp before she discovered we had gone. Then she sat down and laughed though she was sore vexed also. For had not the presbytery in the spring passed a solemn resolution that no Christian should enter the heathen camp on pain of censure of session or presbytery. And here were two ministers, guests of the Mission House, one of whom was present in presbytery when that resolution was passed and besides was in supervision of all the mission work, and the other ignorant of that resolution yet on the impulse of the moment no doubt would have gone if he had known it, here were these two white ministers sprinting across the fields as hard as they could go to watch heathen festivities which had always been a snare to their Indian brethren.

Save for that I have never regretted that I went and saw what I did that afternoon. Never would we see the like again for that was the last time the government permitted such a gathering of wild Indians. In and out of that heathen camp we went and saw all the devilish glamour and savage gorgeousness that covered every kind of wickedness that human mind can invent. Always the somber beat of the tom-tom and the hi-yi, ki-yi, of the Indian dancers in their teepees or around their campfires. There was the gambling going on incessantly; warriors dressed in sweeping eagle feathers riding on horses with silver mounted trappings; women in their gay blankets and highly colored handkerchiefs around their heads and daintily embroidered moccasins on their feet forever on the go or busy about their teepees; children and dogs were everywhere.

But perhaps I prized most of all my glimpse of old Chief Joseph, the famous war chief of the Nez Perces, who conducted one of the most masterly retreats of all history in fleeing before Generals Howard and Miles; and then only through treachery was he captured with his band in the Sweetgrass Hills of Montana. He was now old and living by the grace of the government on a reservation near Spokane. By the grace also of that government he was permitted to be at this camp. His pursuit and capture after a trek of nearly a thousand miles is one of the most interesting chapters in Indian annals. We will have more to say about him again.

When we returned to the Mission House, Miss McBeth met us with rather a half guilty and half amused smile. She had a great sense of humor and every now and then would burst out laughing as she described her sensations when she saw that old minister and the young one streaking it hot footed across the fields to the heathen camp. She informed us that some of the Indian ministers and elders had been there to talk with her about it and said they intended to bring charges against us before presbytery the next spring for violation of the resolution made that spring that no Christian should go to the heathen camp any more.

That was the first time I had heard of such a resolution and I was much disturbed by it. Mr. Adair, however, didn't take it so seriously. He informed Miss McBeth that she was as much to blame as we were for if she had not loaned us her field glasses we would not have become so interested as to want to go. With much laughter she acknowledged her guilt. However the Indians did bring it up before presbytery the next spring, and having acknowledged our fault, the moderator as gravely as possible reprimanded us, though Mr. Adair still insisted that Miss McBeth should be included for loaning us her field glasses. Never again did the Indians have occasion to find fault with either of us. Miss McBeth tells the story in her interesting book "The Nez Perces Since Lewis and Clark" kindly omitting the name of the old minister which was Mr. Adair, and the young man from the east which is myself.

A Great Communion Service

After a week spent in a most delightful way at the mission house and camp-meeting where for the first time I had the privilege through an interpreter; where also I so thoroughly enjoyed the great communion service on the following Sunday when more than five hundred Christian Indians and a score or more of whites, took the bread and cup from the hands of grave and dignified elders to whom they had been given by equally grave and dignified ministers, I returned to Nezperce greatly heartened. I rode back with some of the Kamiah Indians on their way home miles further on. I felt utterly humbled and insignificant after seeing the results of the work done by the Spaldings and the McBeth sisters among the Nez Perces.

With what reverence I stood by the grave of the Spaldings in a fenced burial plot on a bench above the Clearwater close to where the Lapwai empties into it. It is close to the site where they had erected their log mission house and commenced their work sixty years before—they are celebrating the hundreth anniversay as these words are written. An old apple tree was still standing sprung from seed planted by Spalding. Near by stood the Lapwai Indian church a fair sized frame structure and a congregation of two or three hundred souls. It was my privilege to preach in it afterward through an interpreter. The Board of National Missions have in this year rehabilitated the old church at a cost of ten thousand dollars in commemoration of the one hundredth anniversary of the founding of this great mission by Spalding. What a sowing and what a reaping. What an answer to those five Nez Perces who more than a hundred years ago set out to go to St Louis to find the white man's Book of Heaven. For more than a thousand miles they traveled over mountains, through hostile tribes and across great rivers. Their arrival on such a mission made a great stir. They were wined and dined and feasted but were not given the book.

At last when they were ready to return one of them said in words as significant and almost as familiar as those of the Macedonian man to Paul, "I came to you over a trail of many moons from the setting sun. I came with one eye partly open for more light for my people who dwell in darkness. I made my way to you with strong arms through many enemies and strange lands that I might carry back much to them. I go back with both arms broken and empty. The two fathers who came with us, braves of many winters and wars, we leave them here asleep by your great waters and wigwams. My people sent me to get the book from heaven from the white man. You make my feet heavy with the burden of your gifts but the book is not among them. When I tell my poor blinded people, after one more snow, that I did not get the book, no word will be spoken. One by one they will arise and go out in silence. My people will die in darkness. No book from the white man to make the way plain. 'Kullo' '' (That is all.) And some sixty years afterward I had just witnessed at Lapwai how God rewarded that long hard trek and mighty hungering of the Nez Perces for the Book.

When I had returned to Nezperce after that never to be forgotten week in Lapwai, I spent the days in visiting and getting the work more fully organized. There were few workers to help but such as there were responded nobly. I was cheered also with the good news from wife and baby who were getting along splendidly in Montana and counting the days untill they could be with me. Whenever I thought of that my heart went down into my boots. It was no place for a delicately reared wife with her first born. When I was at Lapwai whenever Miss McBeth introduced me to a group of Indian women she invariably told them about the wife and papoose over in Montana which always brought a warm smile and friendly ''Ah'' from them.

Building a Church

With the work better organized the Sunday services and Sunday school were well attended. Then we began to feel the need of a church building. I went out among the people and business men of the community and secured a subscription of several hundred dollars in money and work and material. Mrs. William Thaw of Pittsburgh, wife of the vice president of the Pennsylvania Rail Road had promised two hundred dollars toward its erection, and the Board of Church Erection had promised five hundred dollars. This was sufficient to erect a neat little building large enough for our needs. What we really should have done was to build a manse first but more about that.

The lumber had to be hauled from Craigs Mountain twenty miles away and was very cheap, ranging in price from ten dollars a thousand for rough lumber to twenty five for finish. Volunteers were found to haul this lumber as subscriptions to the new building and much of it was soon on the ground. A local carpenter and I drew up the plans for the new building. But we were not the only body of Christians to start work on the newly opened reservation. The Methodists with their usual aggressiveness soon sent in two missionaries who also had homesteads of their own. One of them was a big rawboned fellow with a voice like a fog horn. He had been a cowboy in Montana but on his conversion became a minister and was used by his church in its rough and out of the way missions. He was earnest and sincere, a rough and ready speaker, without a particle of education or refinement, crude and overbearing and very jealous in his disposition. The other was a small man of a more refined character and not nearly so aggressive as the other. They established a large number of preaching stations in regular old time Methodist fashion and made their headquarters in Nezperce.

Seeing the preparations being made by myself for the erection of a building, the big fellow and his helper determined to outdo me. They must have up the first building. Gathering together a number of Methodists who had been worshipping with us he induced them to separate themselves from us and organize a congregation of their own. The next step was the erection of a church building. So one Monday morning he started out to the mountains with several wagons intent on bringing back enough lumber to build a church or at least to make a good start at it. In a day or two they came back each wagon heavily loaded. I looked on and smiled t[h]ough I must confess to a certain unchristian feeling regarding the whole affair. It had seemed to me unbrotherly and unfair in the first place to attempt to divide the Christian forces of the community at least for awhile. Then the determination to outdo me in the erection of a church building seemed only a scheme of a low kind to defeat us in our own begun purpose. I held my peace and went on. In a few days the big fellow and a number of his congregation began work on their building. The sills were laid on wooden blocks without rock footing and they soon had the framework up, the roof on, and the sides and ends partially boarded up. It looked as though they would be having preaching there before very long while the stone foundation of the Presbyterian church was just finished. But one hot afternoon in late summer great clouds began to form in the west and hoarse thunder bellowed afar off. Nearer and nearer it came; louder and louder was the thunder; sharper and sharper was the lightning and there was a roar different from anything I had yet heard. Then with a mighty gust of wind the storm swept down on the little town with hail and rain that lasted for an hour. When I looked out after the storm I chanced to look toward the new Methodist building, and saw that the wind had turned it upside down and squashed it like an egg shell. So great was the ruin that they did not attempt to rebuild it for a year or more. In the succeeding months I saw our own building completed with the Methodists sharing in its services.

Along about the latter part of July there was a proposal made to hold a service at Greers Ferry down on the Clearwater River about twelve miles away. Announcements were sent to the people along the river and up into the Weippe country on the other side of the river telling them there would be an all day meeting at the Ferry on a certain Sunday with a basket dinner at noon between services. A number agreed to drive down to the Ferry from Nezperce starting early so as to get there by ten o'clock.

The Two-Horse Shay Breaks Down

Early Sunday morning I climbed aboard a rather shaky looking spring wagon or hack belonging to a citizen of the place and driven by his fifteen year old son. Including his mother and a neighbor woman and another boy there were five of us in the vehicle. I didn't like the looks of it or the light team or the patched up harness but I got aboard trusting we might get through before any breakdown. About eight miles out, crash, went a wheel and we were still several miles from the Ferry. Some other folks came along soon and took the two women and extra boy. Before they came however I saw a house not far away with a tepee beside it, a sure sign that some Indian lived there.

I was told that it was the home of Indian George and then I remembered I had met him at Lapwai at the campmeeting there. He was an elder in the Meadow Creek church. I remembered that all of these Indians had good hacks which they were able to buy with the money the government was paying them for their reservation. I wondered if I might not be able to rent or borrow his hack for the rest of the day and return it the next day. Jumping on one of the horses with the boy driver on another, I rode over to Indian George's place. With considerable difficulty I made him understand our trouble and who I was; that I was the Presbyterian minister at Nezperce whom he had seen at Lapwai and was on my way with some other folks to the Ferry to preach to white folks; that our hack had broken down and that I wished to borrow or hire his hack for the rest of the day.

The old Indian seriously considered letting me have it. But when I went out to get it his wife came out furiously and stood in front of the shed where the wagon was and refused to let me have it. Out of her shrill cries I caught only two words that I understood and these she said over and over "Sabbath Day, Sabbath Day." I was compelled to go back to our little party and report our failure. By this time the other hacks had come along on their way to the Ferry and took the two women and extra boy with them. Throwing my linen duster over the harness of the horse I was riding I rode down to the Ferry in that fashion while the boy driver rode the other one. I was afterward told through Miss McBeth that the only reason I was refused the hack of Indian George was because they thought it was violating the Sabbath by loaning it.

At the Ferry I found about fifty or sixty people gathered together from both sides of the river and from the Weippe Meadows. I preached to them a simple gospel sermon. Some of them had not heard a sermon for many months. Then we had dinner under the cottonwood trees back from the river. It was an interesting spot for it was at the mouth of Lolo creek which Lewis and Clark had followed down a hundred years before when they were searching for a path to the Pacific. And it was on the Weippe Meadows from which many of these people came that day that they first came into contact with the Nez Perces.

After dinner we had Sunday School and then another sermon which the people seemed greatly to appreciate. By this time it was getting toward evening and as the most of us had a long climb up the sides of the canyon on either side some to the Weippe and some to Nezperce and some along the river we began to separate. As I went up that trail horseback with my linen duster as my saddle I was glad that I had come and had the privilege to preach to hungry souls in that hungry place As I went up the trail from the river after being ferried across where it wound through the pines and upward for two thousand feet to the prairie above. I stopped more than once to look at the indescribable beauty above and below and around me. On one bench where I stood for a longer time I could look up and down the river for miles and miles. It was one continuous park of trees and meadows and wooded canyons with the river winding in and out far below. It was a great place for a great congregation to sing the Doxology. One alone could sing it only in heart. So far as I know the services that I held that day were the first to be held for white people on the Upper Clearwater and could learn of none other. Many times Spalding and the Indian ministers preached to Indians along there but never to whites. Since then I presume hundreds of sermons have been preached along the river there and I suppose a thousand white people have heard and believed.

A Primitive Home

About the middle of August my wife and the baby and my wife's mother who would not be separated from the baby came from Montana to be with me. Naturally I was excited and happy. I was to see my wife and baby that I had left when the baby was only a few days old a couple of months before. I wanted them there with me but where should I put them? There was only one available building in the town and that was the empty store building I was already occupying. It had two or three rooms at the back where the proprietor had formerly lived. I furnished these as well as I could but even then I knew it was only a makeshift. When it rained the street in front was but a mass of sticky mud and the water would leak through the roof in several places and the floor be a messy looking place of muddy foot prints and little pools of water. If it was dry the dust of the streets would blow in at the cracks and doors and settle like a black pall over everything.

I rented a team and hack with which to drive to Lewiston to meet my wife and baby and the mother. At that time the Palouse Branch of the Northern Pacific had not been built into Lewiston but stopped at Juliaetta some twenty miles up the Clearwater and Potlatch Rivers. All passengers and freight for Lewiston came to Uniontown another terminal of the Palouse Branch at the southern end of the great Palouse plateau and only twelve miles from Lewiston. Lewiston was then a town of about fifteen hundred people at the junction of the Snake and Clearwater Rivers and head of navigation on the Snake. Small steamers ran between Lewiston and Riparia sixty miles down the Snake receiving freight and passengers there from the Oregon Short Line which ran between Portland and Spokane and crossed the Snake at that point. Lewiston was the supply point for all of that hinter land of the Nez Perce and Camas Prairies and for the Weippe and Pierce City mining country and for the Salmon River stock ranges and mining camps beyond. It had almost a tropical climate sheltered as it was between mountains.

Uniontown as we have said was the nearest railroad point to Lewiston. It was twelve miles distant and lay twenty five hundred feet above it. It was reached by means of a stage and freight road that crossed the Clearwater River on a ferry and then wound upward like a serpent's trail back and forth on the face of the canyon slope, crossing ravines and gullies and sometimes skirting the edge of a cliff over which stage and freight wagon often hung in perilous danger of going over altogether; and if it did go over it would go rolling down to the bottom hundreds of feet below. Whoever went over that road never forgot the thrill of it.

I went up on the stage from Lewiston and held my breath more than once as I was sure we were going to the bottom. What would it be like coming back that night with the wife and baby and mother? Yet I was entranced by the wonderful view that I got as we climbed upward. More and more of the hills above and beyond Lewiston stretching away untill they were merged into the tree fringed summit of Craigs Mountain; or in another direction to the distant horizon of Oregon; or far yonder to the Potlatch country I had crossed a couple of months before; or westward where the old stage road into the Walla Walla country wound through dusty sage brush plains. Below us were the Clearwater and the Snake with Lewiston nestling at their junction amidst its setting of Lombardy poplars and cottonwood trees. The little steamer from Riparia was just tying up at the wharf. After forty years the thrill of that afternoon ride still stirs my blood.

A Happy Family Reunion

The stage reached Uniontown a little while before the train was due and I took advantage of it to look around a little. I dont remember much about it as my heart was taken up with the thought of wife and baby and mother soon to arrive. I only remember the stage office and hotel near by. I only remember the town as a dingy little place in its somewhat dreary setting among the Palouse hills. It wasn't long before the train pulled in and great was the pleasure of all of us to be together again. Of course my wife and mother could scarcely wait untill we got to the hotel where we expected to eat before going down the hill to Lewiston in order to show me the wonderful girl baby that in two months had become such a lusty youngster. No such baby had ever been born. And when, man fashion, I didn't enthuse as much as they thought I should they declared that I couldn't appreciate such a baby and that my capacity in that line was utterly nil.

After a good supper the stage swung around to the hotel. With many a flourish of whip and guarded profanity thrown in for a little spice the driver skillfully brought it to a stop. Both stages were heavily loaded for it took two to haul the passengers and a third wagon to haul the baggage. The mail went down with the passenger stages. That was a paying stage route in those days. When we climbed into the stage my wife's mother insisted on holding the baby claiming that neither I nor my wife had intelligence enough to do so. There were four lithe wiry little cayuses hitched to that stage and at a word they were off. Down the mountain side they tore the driver now and then encouraging them with a sharp word or snap of the whip but keeping his foot on the brake every step of the way.

It seemed sometimes as if we would go off the grade at some of the sharp turns but always they held to the road while the stage bounced from side to side or up and down according as they swerved this way or that or struck a rock or crossed a ravine. We came down to the river without a mishap and soon were being ferried across. From the ferry we dashed up with the usual flourish to the old Raymond House which in its day had housed many a notable man and woman and was owned and run by one of the old families of the city. Compared with modern hotels, it was an insignificant affair but compared with the structures for public entertainment in the little frontier towns such as Nezperce it was a palace.

After spending the night there in comfort, the next morning all of us wife and baby and mother and myself started in the open hack I had hired to drive through to the reservation town some seventy five miles away. My heart though glad was very anxious also. Were we not leaving the comforts of civilization behind us and all that the others had known in former years of culture and refinement? It was particularly hard on my wife's mother who had known the plenty and even luxurues of a Canadian home and had sailed the seas with her Captain husband and had occupied the captain's well kept cabins and the comfort of foreign hotels. And now she was seated in an open spring wagon, drawn by indifferent ponies, traveling over rough roads under a blazing sun and bound for a life she had never experienced. And she would hold the baby for it was the baby that brought her.

Meeting a Forest Fire

Sometime in the afternoon we reached Lapwai and the blessed comfort of Miss McBeth's mission house. Here we stayed all night and never was a night more greatly enjoyed. This was the last touch of comfort and sympathetic hospitality on the way. The next morning we started again for the new little frontier town still sixty miles away. As we slowly climbed the slope of Craigs Mountain I tried to interest my wife and her mother in the scenery. But the ride was so painful, the road so rough, and the baby so great an object of solicitude that their interest in anything else could not be aroused. We got our dinner at Holt's Ranch of which I have spoken several times. Also the horses got a good feed and water. Then after dinner we drove slowly up the mountain side untill we reached the summit and beautiful timber that stretched away in grateful shade for ten miles to the edge of the prairie beyond. As we drove over the winding road at good speed through this natural park I saw ahead of us a forest fire on both sides of the road. Looking more closely I saw that it was only the grass and underbrush that was burning though a few trees had caught fire. With great anxiety I drove ahead through the flame and smoke for a couple of miles.

When we were safely through I was glad, more glad than I can say. It might easily have been otherwise if there had been a wind. And the wife and mother had been very heroic and the baby slept through it all. And so went on mile after mile of the weary way, past Forest, past Kippen, out over the beautiful rolling prairie, over the hill tops and across the hollows, nearer and nearer we came to the end. Home I can not call it. Houses and lands had I none. Only a rented store building and a needy place where I hoped to do service for the Master. What a place materially into which to bring wife baby and mother.

We did not go directly to the store building where we expected to live. The merchant and his good wife, with whom I had stayed when I first came untill I had found a room, had insisted that I bring my family to their home when I returned. And it was very fortunate that I took them there when we reached the end of that long hard day. It was such a clean, comfortable, and homey place. The merchant's wife had prepared a substantial supper of fried chicken, mashed potatoes and gravy, and delicious bread and butter and coffee. How we ate and how comfortable the beds on which we slept that night. It gave my wife and her mother some comfort to know that they were not altogether beyond the reach of civilization.

A Serious Housing Problem

The next day we went to our own place in the store building and it was quite a change from the comfortable home of the merchant to the somewhat dreary store building. However it was not long before the housewifely skill of the wife and mother changed even the appearance of this dreary place into one very comfortable and homey. But as the days went by it became increasingly evident that we could not live in this building when the fall rains and winter snow came. That sooner or later I would have to take them to some place where they would be comfortable at least. After a couple of months I decided to take them to Lewiston and get a little cottage for them for the winter while I would remain on at Nezperce and visit them as often as I could. It made quite a little dissatisfaction in the community when I decided to do this. Protests were made both to myself and the home mission committee of presbytery by the little congregation though I think it was mostly the merchants with whom we traded.

I didn't like to do it any more than they liked to have me do it. I knew that our motives would be misjudged and that it would more or less hinder our work. I took it up with the home mission committee of presbytery of which Dr. D. O. Ghormley of Moscow was chairman also with Dr. Thomas M. Gunn synodical missionary. They didn't like it any more than I did. Nevertheless they were very reasonable. They knew that a man with a family could not do efficient work in a place like Nezperce unless he had a decent place in which to live. So we all decided reluctantly that the move should be made. The great mistake was in not providing a comfortable living place for the missionary and his family at the very beginning of such raw work. A manse should have been the first building erected. They did it for their foreign missionaries but nowhere on the home field was it ever done. It was a great loss to the church for many a capable man with capable and consecrated family turned away from many a field that for that very reason became a loss to the church. They even chose much less promising fields because there was a manse.

Sometime in the early fall I took my family down to Lewiston where we found a cosy little brown cottage of three rooms in what was called Poe's Orchard. Here I established them and there were a splendid lot of people all around them and where they spent a comfortable winter. I visited them as often as I could which was not often as I was busy up there with my new church building and general missionary work. The Sunday School missionary had given me his little gray cayuse for use during the winter and I made many a call at settlers' shacks which I could not have done otherwise. Amony my close friends and companions was a retired colonel of the regular army who had taken up a homestead adjoining the townsite. He was a picturesque character with long white hair curling down upon his shoulders and with his military bearing and military cloak thrown around his shoulders. He belonged to an old New Jersey family and was a graduate of West Point. He had a family but they were not with him at the time.

Periodic Drinkers in the Community

But he was a periodic drinker, in the same class as the merchant of whom we have spoken. Though the government did not allow liquor to be sold or to be brought on the reservation these periodics found a way of getting it and every now and then they would get together in the store or out at the colonel's homestead and have a glorious time of it. The old colonel had a factotum, an old army soldier, whom he called his orderly and who did not have a great deal of intelligence but waited on the colonel with great faithfulness. He was also one of the men who made up the periodic drinking parties.

All over the townsites were shallow wells or water holes that the citizens had dug for domestic use in watering their cows and horses. These were from eight to ten feet deep. They were open and any one might stumble into them on a dark night. One night, Murray, the Colonel's factotum, was steering him home after one of these drinking parties. Both were drunk. Undesignedly Murray steered the colonel into one of these water holes. "Plop" he went into it and the icy water came nearly up to his neck. He began to cry lustily for help and Murray reached down to help him out but he was too drunk to get the colonel up. When he had him half way up he would let him go "plop" back again into the icy water. After several attempts at this some one passing by heard the old colonel say "Damn it Murray you will let me drown." Then the passer by with great shouts of laughter came and helped him out. With great glee he told it the next day. But the colonel was sober for a long time afterward.

Just to show the varied character of my missionary work and the problems that arise among the settlers on a new project I will tell an incident that occurred that fall that affected and divided the whole community. One of the elders of our church was the Kentuckian of whom I have spoken. He was a man of good moral character and generally faithful to his Christian and churchly duties. But he was rather close and grasping and drove a hard bargain. He was the butcher of the community and had a partner who was a fair sort of a man but covetous. A colony of Dunkars had settled in and about the town and as usual were a thrifty people. Among them were two ministers. One had taken a quarter section adjoining the townsite. The other had taken a quarter section farther out but still within easy distance. They seemed to be both excellent men and good citizens.

Dealing in Frontier Justice

In some way or another our elder and his partner had heard a rumor that these two men still owned land or were reputed to own it back in Iowa. According to the U.S. land laws that would debar them from making entry here. Feeling sure of their ground our elder and his partner moved on to the claims of the two ministers and filed counter claims in the U. S. Land Office at Lewiston. By this time the whole community was divided and in a ferment. The case was heard in the Land Office but for some reason or other the Commissioner could not decide it. It was about to be taken before the U. S. District Court when one of the ministers came to me and asked me to arbitrate the matter inasmuch as all were Christian men and the Dunkars by the articles of their faith were forbidden to go to law. I said I had never done such a thing but if all were agreed and would come to my room on such an evening I would hear the matter.

At the appointed time all were present. After prayer for guidance I heard the statement of both sides. I thought of a possible way out. Turning to the minister whose claim lay nearest the town and which had been jumped by our elder, I said "Mr.—— you have a lot and shack down here on the townsite. It is possibly worth a hundred dollars. Would you deed that house and lot to Mr—— if he will get off your claim and leave you in peaceable possession?"

Though he was not inclined to do it yet with fine spirit he said he would. Turning to the elder I said "Will you accept the deed to this lot and shack and get off Mr.——'s claim and give him peaceable possession?" He said he would and they shook hands on it.

I turned to the other minister whose claim had been jumped by the partner of our elder and said "Mr—— would you be willing to give this man a hundred dollars if he will get off your claim and leave you in peaceable possession?" He instantly said he would. Turning to the other man I said Will you accept one hundred dollars and get off his claim and give him peaceable possession?" He said he would and they shook hands on it. That ended the matter. The next day the whole transaction was finished by the transfer of property and money. Everything was carried out as agreed and never after was there a hint of trouble. A matter that had divided the community for weeks besides the expense to the contestants and the bitterness engendered in their hearts was set at rest forever by the Scriptural rule that Christian brethren should settle their differences between themselves and not go to law before unbelievers. One of the Dunkar ministers came to me the next day and wanted to know what I would charge for my part in the matter. "Why," I said "I couldn't do a thing like that. All of us came to the settlement of it as Christian brethren and not as advocate and clients. I would never feel right if I accepted anything for any part I had in it." He went away thanking me and I know he had respect for me.

The Town's First Funeral

Another incident that happened that winter will give some idea of the very primitive and undeveloped life of the community. There was a young married couple living in one of the shacks of the town. They had come with the colony of Dunkars from Iowa to find a home if possible on this great reservation. The wife was a niece of the minister whose claim I had just arbitrated. She had tuberculosis and about December she died. That was the first death in the community. There was no undertaker in the town as yet. The nearest was at Cottonwood a small town on Camas Prairie some twenty miles away. There being no undertaker the carpenter who was finishing up our church and I made a casket out of some good finish lumber. We gave it to a couple of women who covered it first with plain black cotton and over that draped some fine black crepe; they covered the inside with fine white muslin and when it was finished it was very good looking indeed. For handles I went to the harness maker and had him make six black and rounded handles which were fastened with strong screws to the casket.

It really was as good as many that were made in regular factories. It looked well and was quite substantial. No cemetery having yet been provided for I helped a committee select such a piece of ground. I also helped to dig the grave for the young woman. I assisted the Dunkar minister in the funeral services in our church and then helped to fill up the grave. It is not likely that I should ever forget that first funeral service in that new community and the great crowd that came. There were several others that winter but none as dramatic as this. The doctor of the community who was a drink addict added to the drama of it by drinking the bottle of embalming fluid gotten at the little town twenty miles away. His whisky poisoned system refused to be shocked by the new concoction and went about his business as usual.

And the work went on apace. Steadily we were gaining and by Christmas we were preaching regularly in the new church building. We held our first Christmas exercises in it but first I must tell of an experience that I had about the middle of December or thereabouts. I had visited my family in Lewiston a few times and was always lothe to leave them there. Though I didn't know it I was soon to have an opportunity of having them with me but was to be disappointed as we shall see. About fifteen miles away on the other side of a deep canyon called Lawyers Canyon on Camas Prairie was another little town called Denver. In it was a small Presbyterian church ministered to by an energetic and capable minister of the Cumberland Presbyterian body. He served that and other points. He wrote me a couple of weeks before Christmas and asked me to come over and help him in a week's meeting. I wrote that I would gladly come.

At the appointed time I rode over on the tough little cayuse that I used in my missionary work that winter and the meeting commenced with considerable enthusiasm. But in a couple of days I received a letter from Dr. Ghormley, chairman of the home mission committee of presbytery and forwarded to me from Nezperce telling me to go to Grangeville at once and organize a Presbyterian church and remain there. Grangeville was a hustling little town of twelve or fifteen hundred people a county seat and mining center nestling at the foot of the montains about twenty miles from where I then was.

A Mountain Drive in Winter

The order to go to Grangeville came as a complete surprise. To be sure I had called the attention of the committee to the place. I had discovered it for the first time one day when riding out to visit some settlers at the edge of Lawyer's Canyon. I saw it across twenty miles of prairie on the other side of the canyon looking white and clean against its green background of pine covered mountain. I made inquiries concerning it and heard many good things about it. It seemed to me a good point to establish a Presbyterian church and I so wrote the committee. But I had no thought of leaving nor did I ask to leave Nezperce not untill the following April at least.

But now the chairman of the home mission committee had told me to go there and remain and not go back to Nezperce. I was greatly pleased for it meant that I could have my family with me. After talking it over with Mr. Perkins the minister whom I was helping in the meeting I decided to have my family come up immediately and go on to Grangeville and get settled before Christmas. It was seventy five miles from Lewiston to Grangeville and a stage ran daily between the two places. At that time of the year the roads were generally in a frightful condition and the wheels of the stage were often solid with ice and mud. The wife and baby and mother could hardly stand the trip by stage at that time of the year.

Mr. Perkins said, ''Now I have a good hack and a good team of horses standing in the stable doing nothing. If you like you can take the hack and the horses and go after your family and bring them yourself. You can take two or three days at it coming back which will not make it hard for them as you can stop as long as you like at the several stage stations.'' This seemed a good offer and a wise thing to do. I said I would do it. I sent a message to my wife that I would be in Lewiston in a couple of days to get them and take them to Grangeville. When I started out at about five o'clock in the morning the thermometer registered below zero but I was warmly clad and having several blankets I was not uncomfortable. How the wheels sang on the frosty road and how the team was soon covered with the white frozen breath of their nostrils.

At noon I stopped at one of the stage stations for dinner and fed and rested my horses for an hour. I was aiming to make Fontaine's, a stage station twenty miles farther on at the foot of Craigs Mountain, for the night. About half past three or four o'clock I came to the timber belt of Craigs Mountain about seven miles in width and in which there was not a house or building of any kind. There was a comfortable looking settler's shack and outbuildings at the edge of the timber and I was half inclined to stay there for the night if they would let me. But I was anxious to get as far as I could that day and decided to push on to Fontaine's and the team seemed all right. It was only ten miles farther, seven miles through the timber and three miles down the slope of Craigs Mountain. That morning as I started out Mr. Perkins had said, pointing to the horse on the near side, ''Now that mare has been showing signs of colic lately when I have driven her. If she shows any signs of it today just keep driving her on and she will get over it.''

We had not gone more than a couple of miles in the timber when I noticed she was showing signs of colic. Remembering what Mr. Perkins had told me I kept driving her on. But she got worse instead of better. After an hour or two of the most agonizing efforts to keep her going which harrowed my feelings as much as the colic hurt the horse I came to the edge of the timber on the other side. Off to one side of the grade leading down to Fontaines I saw a settler's shack and realizing that it was impossible to go farther with my sick horse, I drove up to the door, got out, and knocked. A thinly clad woman answered the knock and as politely as I could I explained the situation as regards the sick horse and asked if I might stay all night. She answered gruffly that it was impossible to keep me. I told her it was impossible for me to go on and that she must keep me some way. I told her I was a minister of the gospel and perfectly reliable. Which didn't help much. She finally told me that I could put my team in the barn and sleep there myself if I wished. So I drove out to the log building she called a barn and unhitched my team in the dark. I found a place to water them and put the well one in the stable and fed it some ground barley I found there. The sick one I put outside in the corrall where she would have room to roll. There wasn't a thing I could do for her which harrowed my feelings.

Sleeping in a Barn

I went to the house and asked if I could get something to eat. The woman asked me into the kitchen and gave me an old chair to sit on. She then began to get supper for me and her children of which there were five of all ages and scantily clad. She explained that her husband was away and that she had a very sick mother in the next room. There were two rooms down stairs and an attic above reached by a ladder. The old grandmother lying in the next room was sick unto death as I afterwards learned. The supper consisted of fried potatoes, stale bread, and black tea. When I had eaten I went out to look at the sick horse but found her no better. When I came back I went into the room where the sick woman lay and tried to talk with her but found her too sick to listen. I sat there talking to the other woman and her family for a couple of hours.

I asked if I might not be allowed to sit in the kitchen all night but with considerable embarrassment she said she could not allow that but that I could sleep in the barn if I liked. There being no help for it I went out. The night was clear and cold and the thermometer somewhere near zero or below. The moon and stars were shining brightly. I went into the barn having taken the blankets out of the hack. I put one of them down on some hay and got a sack of barley for a pillow and laid down in my overcoat and put the other blanket over me. Mr. Perkin's dog had followed me that day and came and laid down beside me. I could look up through the great holes in the clapboard roof and see the stars shining overhead. Out in the corrall I could hear the sick horse groaning and rolling on the ground. Occasionally the other horse would give a snort. I dreamed of warm firesides and comfortable homes. I thought the night would never end. My whole body ached and hurt and my heart was sore troubled about the sick mare. There was not a thing I could do but listen.

A Dead Horse and a Wild Cayuse

But morning came at last as mornings have a habit of doing. I heard the woman in the house getting breakfast and there came the smell of it. I got up from the place where I had lain all night. The dog got up and stretched himself. The well horse nickered for some food and I gave it some ground barley and hay. I took some to the sick mare but she wouldn't touch it. I went into the house and washed myself in a rusty basin and wiped on a very dirty towel. Then I sat down to a breakfast of fried potatoes, stale bread and black coffee. After breakfast I thanked the woman for my lodging and paid her some money for the same. It was evidently the first money she had seen for a long time. Then I went out watered and harnessed the horses and hitched them to the hack and started down the mountainside to Fontaines. I had gone but a short distance when I saw that the sick horse was about to lie down with me. I jumped from the hack and catching her by the bit forced her to stay on her feet untill I had stripped the harness from her and got her free from the hack. I then let her lie down and she never got up. She died in the road.

Here was a great predicament. What could I do? I drug the hack out of the road and taking the well horse with the harness of the other I walked down to Fontaines. I paid him to go back and get the hack and drag the dead horse out of the road. When he came back I asked him to let me have another horse with which to drive to Lewiston. He said that he didn't have one but that there was a rancher a little farther down who probably would let me have one. I went down to see him and he let me have a little cayuse that had not been worked for sometime and tricky as you make them. I suspect that the rancher had a good laugh when I marched away back to Fontaines with him.

After dinner I put the harness of the dead mare on him having to adjust it with great care. I hitched both horses to the hack. The tricky little beast didn't approve of things at all. He stood on his hind leges, made himself into a rainbow, and performed generally and in toto as such a beast could be expected to do to the great delight of Fontaine and all of his crowd. But we finally got started down the road, the big horse on the other side of the tongue literally dragging the little cayuse for several miles. Finally after he had become tired of being dragged and of breaking through the frozen surface of the road to the soft mud underneath, he concluded to behave himself and do his duty as a good horse should. He was a mighty tired little animal without a kink in him when we rolled into Lewiston about seven o'clock in the evening.

One thing was sure. I wasn't going to take my family back over that road. I would not go to Grangeville but stay on at Nezperce the rest of the winter untill the spring meeting of presbytery. I sent the hack and well horse of Mr. Perkins back to him by a freighter who was freighting into Grangeville, also the cayuse I had borrowed from the rancher coming down. After a day or two's visit with my family I rode back up to Nezperce with a young man who had come down for a few days on a business trip. And I had [a] dead horse to pay for. There have been lots of them.

A New Church with a Bell

The remainder of the winter I spent in Nezperce while my family stayed in Lewiston where they were very comfortable in their little cottage in Poe's

Orchard. We got the new church building in Nezperce finished by the first of the year and held services in it every Sunday. A Ladies Missionary Society in Ohio sent us money to buy a bell which we did and hung it in the tower and had the pleasure of listening to it ring out over the town and prairie every Sunday. We had the work also well organized. It was a far cry from that first Sunday when I preached in an empty store room to people as homesick as myself.

As spring drew on I got into correspondence with the chairman of the home mission committee of presbytery relative to a change of fields. He was not inclined first to listen, saying that I had not gone to Grangeville as he had ordered me to do, that it was too soon for me to be asking for another change, and that it might grow into a habit with me to want to change. But I convinced him that such was not the case. As for Grangeville he knew the reason as well as myself for my not going. As for Nezperce it was really impossible for my family to live there under the circumstances existing there nor was it right or conducive to successful missionary work for me to live in one place and my family in another as we were doing. So he offered me Kendrick and Juliaetta of which I will have much to say in another chapter.

I want to finish the story of Nezperce before leaving it altogether. Two or three months after we had gone to our new field, one evening there came a knock at our door in Kendrick shortly after the mixed train from the main Palouse Line at Pullman had pulled in. I went to the door and there stood a young man, tall and slender, a little stooped, pale and bespectacled, gentlemanly and courteous in bearing, whom one would immediately recognize as just being out of school. He introduced himself and said he had come to take charge of the work at Nezperce and had been told to stop off and talk with me about it. I invited him in and soon saw that he was no ordinary person. I liked him from the moment I saw him and have kept on liking him from that day to this. My family also liked him exceedingly. In the years to come he was a frequent guest in our home and we were always delighted when he came.

He stayed a day or two with me and I told him all about the field, all that was good and all that was bad; that it was a great opportunity for any man especially at that time for a young man who was as yet single as living conditions were not yet conducive to successful living and work to a man with a family. He seemed greatly interested in what I told him and went on to Nezperce in a fine enthusiasm of finding a great opportunity and pleasure in the work. He was a graduate of Grove City College and of Western Theological Seminary. He was there for two or three years and in that time rode horseback over the prairie and knocked at the door of every settler round about; he was a friend of every man and every man he met was but another opportunity to win one more to Christ. The church grew and prospered and every one had confidence in him. So fine was his work and reputation that he was called first to one church and then another in the Pacific northwest, then to become financial secretary of the great First church of Seattle, and eventually to become the well known financial secretary of the Board of National Missions, the Rev. John A. Rodgers, D.D., from which position he has just retired by reason of the age limit. The Board gained a great secretary but it lost a greater missionary.

For Lack of a Manse

The history of the Nezperce field after Mr. Rodgers left it is not flattering nor is it easy to write about it. The men who followed were not the kind of men needed there though they had fine missionary spirit and made good elsewhere. They did not stay long. There being as yet no manse conditions were as unsuitable to their families as to mine. And so they left as soon as they could get away. The church became discouraged because of the frequent change. Some of the most useful and prominent members died and others moved away so that in a few years it was disbanded. The church building was sold to the Methodists and at this writing serves as a community hall having been enlarged for that purpose. From that day we have had no congregation there. It was mostly due to the lack of a manse at the beginning so essential to the development of the work in a new community. Our ministers, educated in our sometimes luxurious seminaries, are not fitted for such work, and indeed look askance at it. And if they are ever so willing they are lothe to subject their refined wives whom they generally marry to such conditions. It takes men of the type of Marcus Whitman and Henry Spalding and their wives, Narcissa Whitman and Eliza Spalding, for great pioneer work. That great and fertile reservation with its white population should have been all Presbyterian. It belonged to us by reason of the great missionary work of the Spaldings and the McBeth Sisters among the Indians. But we were not worthy and God gave it to another.

PIONEER PREACHER IN IDAHO, II

BY JAMES A. HEDGES

[EDITORS' NOTE: This is the second instalment of the reminiscences of Rev. James A. Hedges, who as a young man, ventured into Montana and Idaho in 1894 as a missionary of the Presbyterian Board of Home Missions. The first section appeared in our JOURNAL for September, 1949, and vividly portrayed life among whites and Indians in the intermountain area in and about Nezperce, Idaho.

The present chapter transports us a few miles northwest from Nezperce to Kendrick, Idaho, a village deep in the canyon of the Potlatch river which is a tributary of the famous Snake River. In the experience of this missionary life was never stagnant. Things happened fast. This narrative of spiritual and material events moves along rapidly. Here we read of unusual weddings and funerals, of the ravages of fire and flood, and of the bell which built a new church — a human document permeated by the spirit of God. It is a thrilling story of the service of this ambassador of Christ in the growing empire of the northwest. This is printed from the manuscript in the archives of the Presbyterian Historical Society.]

We Live in a Canyon

As we have already said, after much correspondence, the chairman of the home mission committee offered me the field of Kendrick and Juliaetta two small towns on the Palouse Branch of the Northern Pacific of which Juliaetta was the terminal at that time. There was a manse at Kendrick which was also the principal business point of that whole region. It was a hustling little town of about four hundred people. It was situated at the junction point where several canyons joined the main Potlatch canyon some just above and some just below the town. These canyons with their several streams of water drained a very large region to the north and south and east and known as the Potlatch country. Roads wound up these canyons until two thousand feet above the town they emerged on a rolling and fertile plateau which was all settled up and stretched away on all sides mile after mile of waving fields of grain and green orchards and vineyards. To the east and north was the great white pine belt of Northern Idaho. It was one of the most fertile and picturesque regions of the Pacific northwest.

The Walla Walla Presbytery met that spring in Kendrick. I rode horseback from Nezperce to Lapwai where I spent the night at the mission house with Miss McBeth. The next day I rode on to Kendrick with about a dozen Nez Perce ministers and elders. We crossed the Clearwater on an Indian ferry and up the river for several miles until we came to the mouth of the Potlatch canyon up which we rode side by side. The cottonwoods along the Potlatch were just beginning to leaf out and Indian farmers along the river and white settlers on the benches above the river were doing their spring plowing. Soft breezes from the Pacific coming up the Columbia and Snake and Clearwater rivers were sweet with the odors of spring. It had been a hard ride of sixty miles I had made the day before from Nezperce to Lapwai and I rode it alone. But on this day I had that splendid company of Nez Perce ministers, Silas Whitman, James Hayes, Mark Arthur, Robert Parsons, Moses Monteith, and William Wheeler, and elders from the various Indian churches. All of these were in the best of humor, laughing and chatting in their own language, sometimes interpreting it when it related to myself. They, with the charm of scenery and weather and the murmur of the river made me feel as though I was on enchanted ground.

After several days spent in the meeting of presbytery I went to Lewiston to bring my family to Kendrick. We were surely overjoyed at the prospect of being together again. We rode up to Uniontown on the stage, thence by rail to Pullman, the junction point where the mixed train for the Potlatch country went on down to Kendrick and Juliaetta. This was the location of the Washington State College, then only a young institution with four or five buildings. In years to come we were to live here where the baby, now only a few months old, was to graduate, a young lady of mature intelligence and fine scholarship. The institution was to grow from a few buildings to twenty or more and the number of students from a few hundred to two thousand or more. So quickly did the great Pacific northwest develop, particularly Washington and Northern Idaho with their fertile fields, their lakes and rivers; their mines and timber; their orchards and gardens; their splendid wealth of young manhood and womanhood.

A Town Six Hundred Feet Wide

Sometime that evening on the mixed passenger and freight train that passed through the Palouse hills of northern Idaho and down through the winding canyon of Little Bear Creek, whose descent was so steep that it fell two thousand feet in twelve miles, we came to the little town at the bottom which was to be our new field. It sprawled along the railroad track from where the Little Bear Canyon and the Big Bear merged into the larger Potlatch until it turned at right angles toward the west following with the railroad the bend and course of the river. It had one main street about a mile long and ending where another canyon emerged from the north into the Potlatch. There were residence blocks at the upper end followed by several busines blocks which were in turn followed by other residence blocks at the lower end. The church and manse were at the upper end about a block up the hillside from the main street. The whole space occupied by the town from the river and railroad on one side to the steeply sloping hillsides on the north was not over six hundred feet in width and in some places much narrower. The canyon on the other side of the river rose up almost in sheer straightness so that there was no room on that side for buildings of any kind.

This was to be our home for seven years. We could'nt see much of it as we came in that night but what we saw was not overly cheering. We went to the hotel kept by a blond faced, blond whiskered, pleasant little Irishman who made us welcome in the cheery Irish way and gave us the best rooms in the house. He was a Catholic but never did Protestant treat me and my family with greater kindness than did he. He had a Protestant wife who became a very earnest supporter of our church in days to come. He kept a bar in his hotel and was as affable in serving the drinks as in serving meals. His hotel was headquarters for timber cruisers and miners and naturally there were some rough customers. But the affable little Irishman had a fierce temper and woe to the man who got o'er rough in speech and conduct. Terrible was the profanity which was heaped on his head and terrible the shillalah which stretched him on the floor. The terror stricken rough neck subsided into silence and the little Irishman became as affable as before and as friendly.

We stayed at the hotel for several days the guests of the hotel man and his wife and were not charged a cent-then. The manse was occupied by the conductor of the train which ran in and out of Kendrick every day. We secured a nice little cottage on the hill above the church building until the conductor could make arrangements to move. We lived here for five months or more. We had for neighbors a fine little Scotch Canadian and his wife and two baby boys. Both were of splendid family and good education. The wife was a very devoted member of the church. She laughingly told me that when I was pointed out to her at the meeting of presbytery a couple of weeks before we came there she exclaimed "O dear me, he'll never do for this place." But she became in her loyalty one of our finest and best workers and unswerving in her friendship to me and my family. Until one day we carried her body up to the little cemetery among the pines on the hillside on the other side of the river. There we laid it tenderly in the grave where the pines might sing a requiem day by day and nature grow upon it a continuous offer of flowers.

Living on Thirty Dollars Per Month

That first summer in Kendrick was hard financially on myself and family. My salary was small only eight hundred dollars and manse. Of this the two fields were to raise four hundred dollars and the Board of Home Missions the rest. There were only sixteen members in one church and about a dozen in the other. There was no one in either place to look after the salary. We went through the summer trying to live on the thirty three dollars a month from the Board. By fall we were considerably behind in our expenses which worried me considerably. One day the Methodist presiding elder came into town to look after his church. He inquired of me what salary I was getting. I told him what I was supposed to get but was only getting about half of it and that from the Board. The next Sunday night he preached a sermon in the Methodist church on the duty of supporting the work of the church financially. In his sermon he alluded to the young minister in the Presbyterian church and how his church had only given him a pittance for the time he had been there.

There happened to be present a good Presbyterian lady, the wife of a prosperous grain merchant who only had been in town for a short time. She was indignant and chagrined and the next day started out to interview the Presbyterians and called together the Ladies Aid Society and in a short time had much of the salary made up with the Aid Society taking it upon themselves to collect it every month. From that time on regularly every month I received the portion of the salary due me from the field. My financial worries were greatly relieved.

Here is as good a place as any to speak of the lodge and my attitude towards it. I am speaking of the lodge in general. I had become a member of the leading lodge of the community soon after coming to the place. It enrolled the best and most prominent citizens. They were a great help to me by standing back of me in the community. Many of them contributed to my support. On the other hand I did not feel that I was winning them to the church and to the Master. I compromised more or less with their attitude toward worldly policies which galled my conscience because I could not endorse their policy and remain true to my convictions. In the end when I went to another field I withdrew from all lodges.

I enjoyed the fellowship of the lodge; I prized greatly the friends I made therein; I appreciated their works of benevolence; many a wife and mother has been made glad by the help of the lodge when the husband and father has been taken; many a child will bless the day when he was put under the care of the whole fraternity in a fraternal home for orphan children and given the training necessary to fit him for modern living. Always have I spoken of these things with the deepest respect. But with all this good to their credit and far more, I felt that there was so much that was not Christian in ritual and work and social program that I could not conscientiously fellowship with them any longer. I found that their members were too apt to think that if they lived up to the ritual of their lodge it would entitle them to fellowship with God. So I withdrew.

The years at Kendrick and Juliaetta were golden years as I came to look back on them in after years. I had ample time for study and had acquired a library of two thousand volumes well selected. I had the confidence and good will of my people and the people of the community. I saw the church in both places triple itself in the years. I had an honorable place in the presbytery and became chairman of its home mission committee. In a peculiar way my life came to be knit very closely with the life of the community. Not so many came into the church on profession of faith as I desired to see. This was always a sore spot in my heart. I was passing now from being a young man towards middle age, strong in body and growing stronger in spirit. It was still a struggle to live within the limits of our small salary and it was very annoying not to be able always to meet all of our bills. The missionary boxes which were sent out in those days were a great godsend to us. We were never ashamed to receive them and the letters of sympathy and helpfulness that came with them were worth as much as were the boxes themselves in making us feel that behind us was a great church that really cared.

Murder Up the Canyon

It was in these years also that second daughter arrived in our home and we were as pleased and excited about it as about the arrival of our first one two years and a half before. From hencefo th our home was full of light and cheer and as they grew older of shouts of childish glee and the eternal questioning "Papa, what are you doing now?" And now as we are facing the sunset hour and our day of toil in the harvest field is at an end these girls now become splendid and well educated and well married and are vieing with one another to make our evening time full of light and peace.

There came also to live with us the father and brother of my wife both of them welcome and oth of them of great help in the home and church. The brother became editor and publisher of the local newspaper taking it over from its former editor and publisher now become head of his lodge in the state and for whom I had done much writing and editing. The father became justice of the peace for several years and when he was not busy with his legal duties helped in the publishing of the paper. At other times being an old sea captain and full of yarns was to be found spinning his yarns in the ears of delighted listeners.

Several incidents of more than passing interest stand out in our lives in this community. The first occurred the first summer we were there. I had a Canadian evangelist helping me in some special services. One morning he and myself got up very early to take a walk up the Potlatch river it being very beautiful at that time of the year. As we neared the upper part of the town and had turned into the road leading up the canyon we met a man on horseback whom I recognized as one of the butchers of the town. He was a great gross looking fellow who looked every inch a butcher. As he came nearer we saw that he was greatly agitated and tears were rolling down his cheek. He stopped to say "good morning" and then continued "Gentlemen, my house is on fire up the canyon and I can not find my wife anywhere. I am afraid there has been foul play and that her body is in the burning building. I am on my way down town for help. Leaving us he went on into town and we walked on up the canyon where now we could see the flame and smoke of the burning house.

When we arrived at the burning building it was almost consumed. A dozen fire companies could'nt have saved it. Looking closely, as near as we could come to the fire, we saw two bodies in the basement partially consumed. They seemed to have fallen from the room above through the burning floor. After this gruesome discovery we walked back towards the town not caring to be summoned as witnesses in the trial we knew must come. And there was'nt anything we knew that would help clear up the tragedy. We met several men hastening out to the fire and talked with them a little about it. In the trial that followed the butcher gave it as his belief that a third man staying with him and his wife had fallen in love with her and had waited that morning until the butcher had started down to his shop and approached her and being angry at her repulses had shot her. Being unable to get away because of a passer by coming down the canyon who testified that he heard two shots at different intervals he set fire to the building and then shot himself. There being no evidence to connect the butcher with the crime he was let go though it was the consensus of opinion in the community that he had shot both the wife and the other man and had set fire to the building to cover it up.

A Terrifying Wreck

Another incident occurred about the fourth year we were here which was one of the memorable tragedies of the Pacific northwest. The Northern Pacific was extending its line up the Clearwater river to a point about seventy miles above Lewiston so as to tap the rich and undeveloped territory on the upper Clearwater. They had extended their line from Juliaetta to Lewiston a year or two before and the Clearwater branch was the last link in their development of that region. They brought down from Spokane great train loads of railroad iron for this extension. Along about the first of December a train of nineteen heavily loaded cars of railroad iron having two engines and two train crews had reached the little town of Troy or Vollmer as it was then called. It was at the head of the steep grade down little Bear Creek canyon twelve miles above Kendrick. The difference in elevation was two thousand feet. It had been raining and freezing all afternoon and the rails were a glare of ice. Fearing to take so heavily loaded a train down so steep and icy a grade, the conductor in charge telegraphed the superintendent in Spokane asking that he be allowed to take the train down in two sections. He was curtly told to go on down with it as it was. He sent back word to order out the wrecking crew to come to the bottom of the hill to pick them up.

They started on down the hill as they had been ordered and scarcely had they gotten out of the yards a mile or two when they lost control of the train entirely. Down it ran increasing in speed and momentum every minute. It shot around curve after curve at every one of which they might have plunged into the canyon if a single rail had given way. They set air and hand brakes but there was no lessening of speed. Faster and faster it slid down the icy rails. One of the conductors and a brakeman cut off the caboose and setting the hand brake on it were able to slide down more slowly after the runaway train. Settlers on the benches saw what seemed a great stream of fire rushing down the canyon. The two engineers knowing they were facing certain death kept up a wild whistling that sounded like the wild yelling of demons in mortal agony. It was a frightful sight and horrible din to all who saw and heard it. It took just ten minutes for that runaway to come down that twelve miles of canyon. If they made the last curve at Kendrick they would have several miles of straight and level track in which to gain control. Who can imagine the feelings of those train crews as with roar and din and flaming fire they rushed on to certain death.

I was sitting in the living room of the manse reading. It was only a few weeks before the birth of our second daughter and my wife and the rest of the family had retired for the night. All at once the sound of the horrid din up the canyon brought me to my feet and I was at once conscious that something awful was taking place. I recognized the sound as that of locomotive whistles mingling with the grating clamor of locked car wheels. I rushed to the door shouting as I ran ''There's something wrong with the train coming down the canyon.'' I opened the door and saw locomotives and great cars of steel shoot out into the river capsizing and piling up one car on top of another. It was a horrid crash that sounded like the smashing at one blow of a thousand buildings. Then there was an awful silence. I ran as fast as I could down to the river and the first thing I saw was a dying man that had been hurled from the top of the train by the sudden crash. He drew his last breath as I reached him. By this time many others had come and searching the wreckage we found three other dead men. Buried under the wreckage was the body of another lying in the water under an engine and not found for two weeks. When the wrecking train lifted the engine from the river bed they found the body of the dead engineer underneath it.

Never was there a more terrifying and as complete a wreck as that. Two or three cars only at the rear of the train remained upright on the track. All the rest were piled in inextricable confusion. Rails were bent and twisted in a hundred shapes and some were sticking downward through the great pile of wreckage as though catapulted from the skies. We carried the dead men to the section house where the next day a coroner's inquest was held. The company was exonerated from all blame but afterward paid the families of the dead men several thousand dollars in compensation. It was small compensation for such a great loss. In those days railroads had tremendous power and influence with judge and jury and witness. It was'nt a fair verdict and because of such verdicts the railroads fell on evil days in years to come.

Two or three weeks after the wreck our second daughter was born of which I have already spoken. Along about the first of January, about a month after the wreck, there came a heavy fall of snow that lay two feet deep on all the ridges round about. Also on the slopes of the mountains where was the **real** source of all the streams that poured themselves down the various canyons into the Potlatch above and below the town but mostly above. They divided the region into various portions called "Ridges" the most of them named after the several streams that ran down on either side of them. After the snow had lain on these ridges for a couple of days a chinook wind began to blow. The chinook wind is a warm wind from the Pacific that will melt a heavy snow in a few hours. In addition there was a heavy rain falling. Water from the melting snow and falling rain began to pile up on the level tops of the ridges round about in the slushy snow, and reaching the point of saturation, broke away, and rushing down the ridge slopes into the several canyons, poured their waters simultaneously into the Potlatch.

The River Goes on a Rampage

Ordinarily this stream could carry off any excess of waters on all of the watershed above without overflowing its banks very far because of the rapidity of its fall. When we first came to Kendrick a couple of years or more before, in walking down the river at the lower end of the town, I had noticed great bunches of ancient drift wood lodged in the forks of a good sized cottonwood tree a dozen feet above the ground. Looking at the distance of the tree from the river, the height of the bank on which it stood and the height of the drift material above the ground, I said to myself, "There must have been some flood sweeping down this canyon at sometime. If it ever happens again it will sweep the town away with it." When I went back up town I walked into one of the hardware stores and asked one of the proprietors "Are'nt you afraid you will get washed out here sometime?" "Why, no," he said. "There never has been such a thing. Beside it could not be. There is such a rapid fall to the river bed that it will easily carry off all excess waters without damage." Then I told him what I had seen in the cottonwood and he said it must have gotten there some other way.

The river had been rising all day swiftly and steadily and by even—it had overflowed its banks as far as the railroad embankment but no one was uneasy. It had been higher than that many times. But there was a weak spot in the embankment where the wreck had occurred a month before. It had not only been weakened by the terrific shock when the train went off into the river but the wrecking crew had further weakened it by digging a hole under the track in which to set a "dead man" for the use of their derrick in lifting cars and material from the wreckage in the river. They had not repaired the embankment here nor riprapped it with stone. With the accumulating waters from above pouring into the various canyons and emptying simultaneously into the river, it began to rise at an alarming rate towards evening and soon was pouring through the break in the railroad and commencing to flow down the main street.

I had started out from the manse, which was on the hillside far above danger, to go down to the doctor's office at the lower end of the town for some medicine that my wife needed. When I got down to the main street I noticed a small stream was beginning to run down it but as no one seemed to be uneasy I kept on wading through water ankle deep at some points and others not so deep. I was perhaps twenty minutes in the doctor's office and when I came out the water extended clear across the street and on to the railroad embankment beyond which the water was rushing on a level with the track. I knew now what was happening. That which I had feared as I stood under the cottonwood tree a couple of years before and saw the debris in its forks was coming to pass. I made haste to get back if I could to the manse on the hill. Where a few minutes before I had passed through water ankle deep it was now knee deep and growing deeper every minute. Logs and branches of trees and various kinds of drift was beginning to float down the street. Horses and wagons were rushing through the waters to rescue men, women, and children from houses that were about to be washed away. There was tremendous excitement now. Men shouting and women screaming and children crying and the ever increasing roar of the onrushing waters.

The Tragedy of the Flood

To this day I do not know how I did it but I finally reached a point where I could climb the hill to the manse. I delivered the medicine and rushed down again to see if I could help save anyone or their property. But by this time the most of the people had managed to reach the hillside on the north of the town and were making their way to the manse and church building which stood high above the raging waters. A fire good and hot was kept going all night long in the church and manse and hot coffee served to all who came. My wife's mother with her usual fine executive ability took charge and made gallon after gallon of it and served it out to the cold and shivering people. There were probably three hundred people in the church and manse that night. During the night we learned of the drowning of three children, members of our Sunday School.

A wagon in which they were being taken from their home was upset by a great log which came plunging down just at the time and the mother and children and driver were all thrown into the water. The driver saved himself and the mother but the children were swept down by the fierce current and lost. Men searched with lanterns all night long the hillside shore along which the runaway stream was flowing if perchance they might find them or their bodies lodged in the bushes growing there. Rumors came all through the night of this one being lost or that one with no certainty of the truth of the report. It was a miserable crowd of people that sat or slept upon the pews and floor of the church or gathered in the manse that night.

When the morning came it was seen that the waters were subsiding. Many who were reported missing or drowned showed up alive and it was learned with a great deal of relief that there was no other loss of life save the three little girls. Men walked out on the hillside to look over the still partially submerged town and ascertain if they could what damage had been done to home or business house. By noon they could walk down the main street whose sidewalks and pavements had been torn up leaving great holes filled with water. Partially wrecked buildings, stores and residences filled with mud and debris, loose property gone that could not be replaced, discouraged and disheartened the people. It was a great opportunity for the manse to bring cheer and help to them. It bound us very close to the people.

The loss of the three children filled the whole community with gloom. A systematic search was made for their bodies in which every able bodied man in the place took part. By the afternoon we had located and found all of them. Two of them still clasped their dolls in their arms. I will not soon forget the funeral of these children on Sunday afternoon. The whole community was present inside and outside the church. As I looked down on the faces of the children as they lay before me in their caskets they looked to be only asleep. Their natural color was still in their faces and they were holding their dolls on their breast as they would when taking a nap. The mother and father sat where they could see them though they were almost crushed by the sight. Neither of them were Christian people and I could only tell them about a sorrow which is not without hope. But the balm which is in Gilead they knew not. Nor so far as I know did they ever find it. The hope that was David's when he lay aside his sackcloth and adorned himself in kingly garments when he learned that his child was dead, saying, "He shall not return to me but I shall go to him" was not theirs.

The Bell That Built a Church

It was not long before the little town had washed itself clean from the filth and mud and repaired its streets and sidewalks, its business houses and private residences, and was going along in the same old fashion in its community life. Church work was often slow and discouraging but there was sure advance. At Juliaetta a new church building was proposed and got under way. It came about in a laughable way. The old one was shabby and inadequate and too far from the center of town. There was a fine old Scotch elder and his wife there at whose home I always stopped when I preached in Juliaetta and that was every Sunday night. Services were so arranged that I preached in Kendrick in the morning and at Juliaetta at night. That satisfied both places and as they were only four miles apart it made it easy and convenient for me. Kendrick had a church bell but there was none at Juliaetta. The people there wanted a bell also. Our old Scotch elder headed the subscription and carried it around for others to sign. He got together a goodly sum and sent for a five hundred pound church bell. Whenever I had said anything to him about the need of a new church building his thrifty Scotch soul rebelled and he would shake his head in displeasure. I desisted knowing it was useless to try for any such a thing when the chief officer and supporter was against it.

In due time the bell arrived and there was great excitement. A day was appointed to place it in the belfry and the whole community was there to see it raised and put into place. But there was one thing the dear old elder forgot. He forgot to get the dimensions of the belfry before sending for the bell. When all was ready and the bell drawn up to be placed it was found that it was too big for the belfry and would'nt go in. Great was the laughter of the crowd and great was the chagrin of the old elder. They chaffed him with their biting remarks until he was fairly ashamed and disgusted. It was then that I slyly and gravely said to him "I dont see any way out of it, Elder, but to tear down the old building or sell it and build a new one." To my unbounded joy and surprise he said "That seems to be the only way out. I'll give a hundred dollars toward a new building." In a short time there was enough subscribed which together with the help of the then Board of Church Erection was sufficient to build a commodious, neat, and up to date little building and sufficient for all our needs. This is the only instance I ever knew where a congregation was compelled to build to accomodate a bell.

The Wedding That Didn't Take Place

There was a very pathetic incident connected with my work in Juliaetta that left a profound impression on myself and community. There was a beautiful young girl attending the high school from off one of the ridges. She was the daughter of well to do Christian parents belonging to the Methodist church. There was no church of that denomination in the town and she attended our Sunday School, Endeavor Society, and church services. She was well liked by all, being a modest, intelligent, and companionable girl. She became engaged to a young man there who was usually well behaved, fairly industrious, and belonged to a good family. They were to be married at the close of her high school course that spring. She had a beautiful graduating dress made which also was to be her wedding dress.

A few weeks before commencement another young lady made her appearance on the scene. She had formerly lived there and had been the sweetheart of the young man to whom this young girl was soon to be married. They got to running around together again until she became frantic with jealousy. In her despair, one Saturday afternoon, she went to the drugstore and bought a small bottle of carbolic acid. She went back to her brother-in-law's home where she was staying and going to her room put on her graduating dress which was also her wedding dress, and writing a note in which she explained why she was doing the thing she was about to do, took the carbolic acid and laid down on her bed and in a few moments she was dead. There they found her shortly after and the note she had written. It gave her reason for the deed and asked that

I preach her funeral sermon and other farewell messages. The whole community was filled with grief and anger.

I never had so hard a funeral before or since. What text should I take, and what could I say? I had preached only one other suicide's funeral. That was for an old citizen of Montana who had lost his property in the panic of '93. He was too old to recuperate and he could'nt stand the humiliation of it. So he shot himself. But the circumstances were different entirely. I finally happened on the command of Jehu concerning the body of Jezebel, "Take her and bury her for she is a king's daughter." It seemed to fit the occasion and what I had dimly in mind to say. I can remember the breathless interest of the large congregation as I announced the text. A quiet fell on them and an intensity of deep feeling as I spoke that could only come from livest emotions. The parents thanked me for the comfort of it and all were profoundly stirred.

Fifteen years after as I stood on the rear platform of the train watching the scenery of Little Bear Creek canyon up which we were traveling, a man whom I did not know came and introduced himself and said "Do you remember the text and the sermon you preached from it that day you buried Miss—?" He went on to say that he had never forgotten it. I said "How could I forget it?" My old Scotch elder declared the text I had used was'nt in the Bible. I had to show him before he would believe. We laid her away up on the hillside beneath the syringa blossoms—the mock orange—when she had been expecting to wear soon the real orange blossoms at her wedding. The sun was bright, the hillside was green, and the orchards in bloom, all fit for a wedding day instead of a burial service. O death, thou hast thy sting. O grave, thou hast thy victory. O sin, thou hast thy conquests.

A Surprising Bridegroom

Probably this would be a good place to tell of a wedding I had, and I had many of them, which stands out as one of the most unique of all of them. It was an ideal October day. The sun was warm and bright just what was needed to crimson the apple and purple the plum. A blue haze hung over the canyons and distant mountains. The air was buoyant sweet with the autumn odors. Up the long grade our wedding party toiled out of the canyon where below nestled the little town of Kendrick between its rampart of hills. Far down [below] us the Potlatch wound its way through its narrow and picturesque valley. The hillside slopes on the opposite side were crimson with sumac in beautiful contrast to the green and gold of orchards.

Idaho's canyons are deep and the roads long and winding that lead out of them to the rolling plateaus above them. There the country stretches away to the foot of the mountains one beautiful rolling plain and as fertile as the Nile. We passed by great wheat fields from which the grain had just been threshed lying out in the golden haze of an October day, the yellow stubble fields being interspersed here and there with green orchards and cosey homesteads. Great red Jonathan and Ben Davis apples peeped out from the yellow and green foliage while the rich purple of prunes contrasted beautifully with the dark green of the prune trees' leaves. Fruit pickers were at work gathering the crimson apples and purple prunes while packers were packing the fruit for market. The end of our journey when we got up out of the canyon lay sixteen miles over there where the blue haze half veiled the pine covered slopes of the Bitter Roots.

Ours was a merry party. The bridegroom was a fine looking, jolly and energetic salesman of musical instruments and whimsical and notional as the proverbial bohemian. He never ceased to entertain us with his dry wit and mirth provoking stories. In the carriage—it was before the days of the automobile—were myself, and the "best man" and "bridesmaid," both from a city farther down the line. They were a fine young couple and looked as though they would like to be the principals at a wedding instead of seconds. They occupied the rear seat while the bridegroom and myself held down the front one. We found it difficult riding sometimes especially when the wheels would go "kerchuck" into an unexpected and hidden dust hole and we would be shaken up considerably.

We almost had a catastrophe at one point going up the narrow grade out of the canyon. We met a heavy farm wagon coming down on which was the broad grain rack peculiar to this region. A large bed lounge was set crossways on this rack. Here was a predicament. The grade was only about twelve feet wide. On the down hillside if a wagon slipped off of the edge of the grade it would plunge down several hundred feet. Fortunate for us we were on the upper side of the grade. The bridegroom who was driving our carriage was equal to the occasion. He drove the carriage to the edge of the grade where the hillside rose up almost perpendicular above us It stood almost at an angle of forty five degrees. Jumping out, with the assistance of myself and best man, he pulled the top over untill it almost lay against the side of the hill. With that, it barely escaped the wagon which had to move at a snail's pace lest some untoward thing should send it over the edge and into the depths below. We all drew a deep breath when it was over.

The wedding was scheduled for half past two in the afternoon. But the bridegroom happened to think of a favorite cousin of the bride who with her husband and family lived but a short distance from where the road emerged from the canyon. He began to wonder if they were going to the wedding. Driving up to their home to inquire if they were going he found the cousin in tears at the prospect of missing it. She had just received her invitation a few minutes before. They could'nt possibly get ready and get there at the time the wedding was scheduled. With great bon homme and a noble gallantry that looked only to the relief of present distress, without a thought of the bride and guests who would be waiting at the other end, the bridegroom said "If you will come we will put off the wedding until five o'clock. That will give you time to get ready and get there. We'll drive slowly so that you may be able to get there about the same time as we do.''

The other members of the party including myself stared at one another in astonishment and with quiet amusement at the easy method of the bridegroom in meeting a present situation and who looked as though putting off the hour of one's wedding was a thing of little consequence. There was many a covert joke made of it and at the audacity of a man who dared to do it without the knowledge and consent of the bride. Deep down in our hearts was the wonder as to what might be the scenes in her home over there among the pines when her lover and bridal party failed to make their appearance. The appointed hour as it lengthened would be one of tears instead of smiles we were sure. There was nothing we could do about it but just acquiesce. We drove onward for a few miles and brought up at noon with a great flourish in front of the rough board hotel of a little town in the midst of the prairie.

The Golden Glow of an October Day

The landlady who kept the hotel was a little bit excited and testy. She was just getting ready to go to a sale in the neighborhood and she did'nt like to be interrupted in her preparation in order to get dinner for us even though she was to be handsomely remunerated. Besides she had also quite a grievance against the bridegroom who it seems had made love to her daughter in order to sell her a piano and had made a success of both. Consequently she did not feel very good to see him on his way to marry another.

The beauties of that afternoon ride after we had eaten and rested and fed our horses in the soft golden glow of an October day who could describe? I was a bit grateful for the delay of the wedding through the enjoyment of that ride. Over there on the hillsides and beside the winding road the sumac made the landscape crimson with its blood red leaves; the yellow foliage of the poplar; the dark green of scattered groups of pine; the grain fields that were yet unharvested in that altitude; the lights and shadows that passing clouds cast on the distant mountains; the freshly plowed fallow ground; the early sown fields of grain that were already green with its sprouting, how could I ever forget it.

Somewhere about five o'clock in the evening we reached the edge of the timber and still had several miles to go to reach the homestead where the bride lived with her father and mother. By this time the cousin of the bride and her family, at whose home we had stopped in the morning and for whose sake the groom had promised to put off the wedding, had caught up with us and all of us together drove through the timber until we came to the place where amidst the pine trees lay the snug cabin and home of the bride. On entering we found there was much amiss. We found that the wedding dinner was already eaten. The bride was in tears and furiously angry as well as her family. Believing that the groom had played her false and having no telephone to the outside world—there were few telephones then anywhere—they and their guests, settlers on adjoining timber claims, had sat down and with as much cheerfulness as possible had eaten the wedding dinner. Most of the guests had left for home with the exception of a few.

It was into such a scene that I found myself to have entered. The groom took the angry bride into an adjoining room and made what explanations he could and all that he could. They called me in and I could do no more than corroborate his story. So also did the relatives for whom the wedding hour had been put off. After awhile the bride dried her tears and got over her anger and began to see the humor of the thing. Midst laughter and tears I joined together these two under the whispering pines and looked down upon by the stars that had so often given their light to betrothal scenes of the humble and the great but none more strange than this. The remains of the wedding dinner was placed upon the table once more and amidst mirth and merrymaking we all forgot the unbelievable act of a bridegroom putting off the hour of his own wedding without the consent and knowledge of the bride.

It being impossible for the guests to go back to their homes that night nor the wedding party to reach the railway in the canyon town where I lived and whence we had started that morning all of us were compelled to stay all night. The cabin was small having only three or four rooms and that meant that all of us would have to sit up all night. But we were well entertained. The bride was a graduate of the musical department of the University of Idaho while the groom was no slouch musician. He was able to play several kinds of musical instruments. Among the guests was an old Swede living on an adjoining claim who had his violin with him. He had been a member of Ole Bull's celebrated company of Swedish musicians. He had taken up a quarter section of white pine timber as did so many others of every class and condition with the understanding that when they proved up they could sell their claims for a fair price to the great timber companies that were then trying to get hold of every acre of timber that yet remained in the northwest. For that reason one would often find cultured and educated men and women away in the depths of the timber far removed from civilization and living on their claims until they could prove up and sell. My wife's father and brother were of these.

The Charm of a Stradivarius Violin

That was how the cultured Swede happened to be there that night as was the case with others. The old Swede had a genuine Stradivarius which had been in his family for several hundred years. When he drew his bow across the strings the mellowness and beauty of its tones wakened in me visions of all of its past years. I could see courts of royal listeners, academies and theatres, church and cathedral, palaces and private residences thrilling with its melody, and now pouring itself out in these aisles of God's first temples where men truly praise him "with stringed instruments and organs." So passed the night with crash of piano and sound of flute and the rich tones of the Stradivarius a most harmonious end to a day of discords. Nowhere could such a dramatic thing happen except amidst the dreamy beauty and wildness and adventurous invitation of the physical glory and majesty of the pine covered hills of Northern Idaho.

Early the next morning they took me down to a point on the Clearwater branch of the Northern Pacific where I purchased a ticket for the home which I had left the previous morning counting the experience one of the strangest I ever had yet one of the most enjoyable. I have never seen that spot in the great pine woods since that night. I have never looked upon the face of bride or bridegroom. Nor have I ever beheld the countenance of any one who was there. Each went his way whithersoever the river of his life turned. I have no means of knowing whether they emptied themselves into a dark unknown or into the great river of the water of life in the garden of God.

I had another experience in the way of a wedding that was rather amusing and over which I have had many a laugh since. One Sunday after the morning service a rather good looking and prosperous appearing man came to me and asked if I would come to a certain home in the town about three o'clock in the afternoon and perform a marriage ceremony for him and a young lady who was a member of my congregation and a niece of the lady at whose home the marriage was to take place. I said I would be glad to come and the gentleman thanked me and went his way. At the appointed time I and my wife went to the home designated and in a few moments the ceremony was all over. The groom asked me what the fee would be and I said "I never make any charge . Whatever you see fit to give will be all right with me." He reached down in his pocket and brought out a twenty dollar gold piece and was about to hand it to me. I could see my wife's eyes begin to twinkle for my wedding fees always went to her. Then the man reached down in his other pocket and brought out four silver dollars. There he stood balancing the gold piece in one hand and the silver dollars in the other. Finally with a great flourish he handed me the four silver dollars and put the gold piece back in his pocket. To my dying day I will never forget the look of consternation on the face of my wife as the man put the gold piece in his pocket. I knew she had it already spent in her mind for the children were needing things pretty badly in those days. I have married several hundred couples in my ministry and the largest fee I ever received was twenty dollars. The usual fee was five dollars and from that down to nothing. So far as I know no child of any of these married couples was ever named for me in fulfillment of a promise that I should be remunerated in this way.

By the Waters of the Potlatch River

I have always been a lover of nature. This Potlatch region had every thing grand and beautiful that the heart could wish. I loved to walk up the deep canyons and sit beside the tumbling streams as they came clear and cold from the snow clad mountains far back. Here was the richest of flora. Here were ferns and syringa; wild roses and golden rod; trilliums and larkspur and geraniums; violets and blood root and may apple and what not. Later on the crimson sumac mingling with the yellow and brown of autumn leaves filled us with delight. Sitting by the waters of the Potlatch one day as they sang their way down the canyon they seemed to be trying to sing me a song and I wrote this little sonnet which I called

THE SONG THE WATERS SING

The rippling waters gliding swift
  O'er rocky bed, through winding glen
Sing me a song of sweet uplift
  A'song of forever, ever, and then.

"Tell you the words they sing to me?"
  Ah, would that I could, the wild sweet words
The choir of waters ceaselessly
  Sing, like the song of springtime birds.

Now far in the depths of the future
  And away in the maze of the past,
From ages to come to ages that were
  A full diapason expressed.

Ah, visions of truth and of God
  In their song came sweetly to me;
And glimpses of kingdoms untrod
  Were mingled with those that be.

"Sing you the song that comes to me?"
  Ah, would that I could, the wild sweet strain
The choir of waters ceaselessly
  Sing as they swirl through the winding glen.

On my way to the General Assembly in 1901 which met in Philadelphia and the first I ever attended, while sitting in the passenger coach with James Hayes, a famous Nez Perce Indian minister, as we drew near Altoona in Pennsylvania, we saw the passengers crowding to the windows to look at something. We asked some one what it was all about. They told us that we were coming to the famous "Horseshoe Bend" and we must not miss it. It would be a grand sight. So we also began to look out to see this famous thing. When we got to it, it seemed so tame in comparison to what we daily saw in Idaho that we both smiled and I said "Why, we see grander sights every day from my study window." "Where are you from?" some one asked. I said "From Idaho." And they began to point us out from all over the car as though we were strangers from some far off land. And indeed Idaho in those days was a "far country." The Alleghenies are very beautiful but they are not grand like the Rockies. We love the one for their beauty but stand in awe of the other.

The Glow of Religion

I must not forget the old fashioned campmeeting and protracted meetings of some of the more fervent and emotional denominations with whose work I came into contact on this field. I mention them here because they were typical of these earnest, elemental, and emotionally inclined brethren everywhere in the west and southwest. In their evangelistic zeal and thirst for the Spirit they often put us to shame. I recall one meeting especially that I attended. It was typical. The tall, swarthy, blackhaired minister, dressed in a long coat of rusty black, pleading in vociferous tones with the more or less concerned sons of Belial before him; the subdued yet sometimes forceful amens of some old men and women in the far corner; the half curious, half serious, and half convicted sinners on the back seats; a sort of half sneer curling around the lips of some and a tear drop stealing down the cheek of another as the message became more tender; all this I have seen duplicated a hundred times in other places.

The dimly lighted interior of that old wooden church; the plain clothing of the congregation; the heartiness with which they sang in unmusical voices but with hearts full of emotion such old familiar hymns as "Alas, and did my Savior bleed" "I will meet you in the promised land" "Amazing grace, how sweet the sound" and many others. All made a deep impression. Then at last, at the urgent appeal of the minister shouting out his invitation, clapping his hands, and standing on the front bench, one woman melted to tears by the fervent singing and invitation stepped out slowly from the congregation and went forward to take the minister's hand and kneel at the rough mourners bench in front of the pulpit. There was a hesitation in all that she did as though unseen hands were holding her back.

The minister urged the Christians to come forward and kneel around the sister seeking salvation. One by one they came and kneeled in a circle about her. One old brother began to pray in a loud voice and he laid hold as it were on the very throne of God in his beseeching for mercy and for forgiveness for the lost soul. Loud "Amen, Lord," "God help her, Lord" and "Open her eyes, Lord" were thrown in by the kneeling men and women. Then an old mother in Israel whose life had [been] spent on the frontier, with wrinkled face and hard wrinkled hands yet with sweetness and peace and content in her countenance lifted up her voice and prayed for the erring mother; that she might be given power to come out on the Lord's side; that her sins might be forgiven; that she might be spared to bring up her family for the Lord. How that prayer poured forth. It seemed to gather up all the experiences of a life lost and redeemed and to spread them out before the Lord in great pictures painted in the homely speech of the frontier but beautiful in its simplicity and faith.

It was then that I saw how the Spirit of the Master could take the homeliest words and make them beautiful; and could take the most commonplace figures of speech and make them glow with fire. Weeping was heard in every part of the room while even the most hardened turned away from his neighbor lest his emotion should betray him. These are the kind of services that among the rough plainsmen and mountaineers and uncultured pioneers helped to keep the west and great southwest from going entirely to the bad and that made law abiding citizens and brought the joy of heaven into homes that had little else. Those home spun preachers were rough and ready. Their interpretation of Scriptures were often far out of the way and crude. They did'nt bring much culture or refinement with them nor learning. But they did bring men into the kingdom of God and did inculcate a wholesome respect for righteousness. They made honest men of thieves; clean spoken men of blasphemers; sober men of drunken wretches; and virtuous women of harlots. What patriot ever rendered greater service? What prophet was made of sterner stuff?

A Type of Frontier Religion

But here is another picture seen all too often in the west and southwest among the uncultured and uneducated men who went under the name of "Preacher." They are the kind that have made this the cheapest title that may be applied to the highest office of the church. It became so cheap that I have refused the salutation of one who called me "Preacher." Also of one who called me "Brother." The simple title of "Mr." means more to me than these. These men held down the pulpits of churches of their several denominations which in their zeal to make converts and multiply the number of their churches and adherents often called such men to become pastors here and there. The occasion of which I write was the funeral of a prominent member of one of these churches. The church bore the honored name of a great denomination which had cheapened itself by planting a church at every cross roads and manning it by whomsoever they could find with a ready tongue no matter what might be the claptrap with which he fed the people. It mattered only that he was sound on certain of the sacraments.

It was an occasion when the whole community turned out, I with the rest. The preacher was a man past middle age, a barber by trade, whom the denomination had picked up boasting that they had won him from another denomination. They put him in charge of this particular church. The body of the deceased woman was brought in and placed before the pulpit. The friends were ushered to the seats reserved for them with the pall bearers and the rest of the congregation crowding the remaining seats or standing up in the rear. The minister took his place in the pulpit. When the Scripture reading and prayer was [were] over what was my amazement to see the minister step to the door just behind and a little to one side of the pulpit open it and spit a great mouthful of tobacco juice out on the ground and turn and come back and take up the funeral discourse. I looked around to see what was the effect on the audience. But they seemed to take it as a matter of course and as not at all out of place.

Such were many of the ministers of that denomination cheapening the name of religion and the ministers of religion.

We had now come to the seventh summer of our ministry on this field. We have spoken of the proposed new church at Juliaetta and how it came about—to accomodate a new bell that could not be fitted to the belfry of the old building. The work on the building commenced that spring and was pushed as rapidly as possible. Somewhere about the middle of the summer my wife and children and myself were spending a few days in Juliaetta camping out and pretending to have a vacation but in reality I was there helping to lay the floor of the new building and such other work that I could do. One very hot day while working [in] the church I happened to look up the canyon toward Kendrick and saw great volumes of smoke pouring towards the sky. I threw down my hammer and shouted "Kendrick is on fire." "Kendrick is burning up." I started on a run for the railroad expecting to run up the track which was a level grade instead of taking the roadway which was hilly. A young man who also had been working in the church started to run with me. When we got to the railroad we found a hand car standing on the track which was not in use. Getting permission from the agent we took it and climbing on were soon pushing our way up to the burning town. The smoke was rolling skyward in dense black clouds.

A Town Burns Down

When we reached the lower edge of the town after a hard push of four miles we could get no nearer because of the fierce heat and smoke. We left our handcar on the track and hurried up the hill on the north side and looking down on the main street saw that it was on fire from one business end to the other. A few residences that stood near the business districts at either end were also burning up. Looking eastward along the hill toward the manse we saw that both it and the church were safe. My wife's mother and father and brother had remained in it while we were away. On the hillside were groups of people watching the blazing hell below seeing their business houses and homes going up in smoke. So they had stood several years before watching the flood sweep them away. The Captain, my wife's father, had saved the city archives and the books of the newspaper office and carried them with great difficulty up to the manse. He barely had time to get them out before the fire swept down on the office. In a few minutes nothing was left but scraps of twisted iron and a pile of ashes.

It was an infernal display of heat and flames. The canyon acted like a chimney through which the wind tore driving the flames in resistless power until every business house, a few residences and warehouses were totally consumed. Never did fire make a completer sweep. Never was a hotter day chosen for such a fire. Never a more opportune time because the water in the town's reservoir was at its lowest stage and no way to increase the flow. The fire started in a large empty hotel building that stood in the center of the business district. Being of frame it was seen from the beginning that the town was doomed. The only thing that the business men could do was to save their books and valuable papers. It being in the daytime no lives were lost.

Great was the discouragement and depression of the citizens. The most of them had lost very heavily. What should they do? Should they arise and build or move to Juliaetta where there was a much better and safer townsite. There they might build up a good sized town. But the location of Kendrick was so much nearer the center of the whole region; roads had already been built into it from the various ridges and markets established so that it seemed the logical thing to rebuild the town where it stood and insure its safety by better and more ample protection against fire and flood. In a few days the most of the business men decided to rebuild and in a short time the canyon resounded to the sound of hammer and saw, of pick and shovel, wagons and trucks hauling the material with which to rebuild. In these months of rebuilding the town was very prosperous and money very plentiful as is always the case when there is plenty of work and good pay. It was jokingly said that the town ought to burn down every few years.

All the hotels and eating places in the town having been burned some of the business men came and asked my wife if they could eat at the manse until other places were provided. She said they could and for two months she fed ten or fifteen a day. Her table soon acquired a great reputation and strangers and insurance adjusters passing through came and asked to be allowed to eat there. She made enough to pay all expenses and our own store bills so that we were all in the clear. It was hard work and worry for her though she had good help and we were glad when there was no necessity for it any more. My wife's brother published a newspaper at Juliaetta as well as at Kendrick. Having lost his plant in Kendrick and all of his stock of paper he got out the first edition of the Kendrick paper after the fire at the Juliaetta office printing it on wrapping paper. It was kept as a souvenir in many homes for years to come.

A Record of Missionary Labors

In the meantime the church building at Juliaetta was completed and dedicated and was generally approved and liked. The work in both places was well organized and prosperous. I would have been glad if the two towns could have been merged together on the Juliaetta townsite being much the best and was beautifully situated. If it had been more centrally situated to the whole region there would have been a merger without hesitation.

But now I was coming to another experience in my life as a home missionary that was to have a profound effect on me and add another interesting chapter to my home missionary experience. I had spent nearly seven fruitful and happy years on this field and there was no reason why I should not expect to spend many more. My people were contented and satisfied. In the community I was chairman of the schoolboard, my wife's father was justice of the peace and very popular, and her brother was editor of the newspaper. I was chairman of the home mission committee of the famous Walla Walla Presbytery— famous because of the missionary labors of Whitman and Spalding begun within its bounds long years before. At every regular roll call of presbytery the stated clerk called the name of "Waiilatpu" the church founded at Whitman's place of labor near Walla Walla and which became extinct by the martyrdom of himself and family and its Indian members. It was famous because of the continuing and splendid work of Miss Sue and Kate McBeth among the Nez Perces and later their nieces Miss Maizie and Elizabeth Crawford. Its roll had more than forty ministers and churches white and Indian. The most of these churches were home mission churches so that the chairman of the home mission committee had much to do in the way of supervision. What a splendid lot were those missionaries and Indian ministers.

There now opened for me the opportunity to go to the second largest city of the state and commence the establishing of a Presbyterian church there. The city was Pocatello one of the principal divisions on the Oregon Short Line running from Salt Lake to Portland. It was a part of the Union Pacific System. The town had a population of about seventy five hundred people with large railroad shops employing a thousand men. More than half of the population was Mormon. The city was on the Old Oregon Trail over which Whitman and Spalding and their wives had come dragging an old wagon after them. Ten thousand others had come that way also. A church had already been organized on the east side of the town, the only church of any denomination on that side. All the others were on the west side including a Congregational which was strong and influential. The Idaho State Academy, now the Southern Branch of the Idaho State University, had just been established on the east side. The church had just been organized by famous old Dr. Wishard for many years synodical missionary of Utah, Wyoming, Montana, and Southern Idaho. It had twenty members and one elder. At Dr. Wishard's invitation I left the field where I had been for nearly eight years and went to take charge of the newly organized work.

PIONEER PREACHER IN IDAHO, III[1]

BY JAMES E. HEDGES

I wish I could forget that first Sunday in the new field. We had come from the tearful farewells of a people among whom we had served for years. Every year added some new link to tie us more surely to them. Through fire and flood; through sickness and accident; through friendship and pastoral service; through preaching and teaching, we had come into very close contact with them. And they had gathered in a great community farewell party to bid myself and family farewell. Then to come as utter strangers among a handfull of people who received us cordially it is true but so few in number and worshipping in an old store building with an upturned apple box for a piano stool; with only a handfull of Sunday School scholars and a superintendent waiting to resign and a baker's dozen at church the outlook was anything but cheering. Besides I and my family were late that morning due to our clock being out of the way. The Sunday School superintendent who was also the ruling elder said surlily as we came in ''You are not making a very good beginning, Sir.''

We worshipped all of that winter in that hall amidst its discomforts, its dreary walls, and its large dimensions which made our little congregation smaller than it was. When we first came we lived in an undesirable house in an undesirable locality because we couldn't get anything else. In a short time we moved into a more comfortable house a few blocks from the State Academy but we had to pay a much larger rental. This cut our salary down to such a degree that it was sometimes hard to make ends meet and to live as we ought to live. The salary from the Board of Home Missions was always promptly paid but the salary from the field was often a month or two behind, sometimes more. It was very trying and discouraging. To the home missionary it was often not a question of living but of mere existence.

In the spring of the following year we began to think of building a chapel on lots that had been given us half way between the business part

---

[1] The new field to which the writer refers at the beginning of this narrative is the Presbyterian Church at Pocatello, Idaho, which had just been organized with twenty members and one elder. Earlier excerpts from these reminiscences appeared in the September and December numbers of the JOURNAL.

of the town and the State Academy. We planned to erect a small chapel on the rear of these lots that we could use as an educational unit of a larger structure we hoped to build in the future. Plans were drawn by a local contractor calling for a building of simple design yet good enough and large enough and convenient enough and good looking enough for the time and needs of the congregation. A building committee was appointed by the congregation. Its chairman was the Sunday School superintendent of whom I have spoken. He had a hardware store and was of course anxious that the contract should be given to a contractor friendly to himself, being desirous to furnish the glass and the paints and hardware for the new building. And all of us wanted him to do so. But he was a little too anxious and did a thing that was not right.

Collusion in a Church Building Contract

Bids were called for by the committee. The contractor who drew the plans put in a bid as did others to be opened on a certain day. When the chairman of the building committee received this bid knowing the contractor was unfriendly to him and that in making up his bid he had figured with another hardware merchant he deliberately opened it found out the amount of it and then resealed it. He made known the amount of the bid to another contractor friendly to himself and friendly to the church. When the bids were opened it was found that the bid of this contractor was just a few dollars under the first. It being very obvious that unfair methods had been used and much as we desired to give the contract to the last bidder both because he was friendly to the chairman of the building committee and to the church yet I insisted that for fairness sake and that the church might gain a reputation for square dealing in the community we should call for new bids.

This of course made the chairman of the building committee and the contractor friendly to him very angry. I lost their friendship and co-operation. Yet I knew I was right. For if a church can not be square in business matters little can it expect to be a model and example for straight business in the world. When the new bids were opened it was found that the bid of the first contractor was much lower than any other and the contract was awarded to him. To my great sorrow the breach between myself and the chairman of the building committee was never healed but rather widened as time went on.

The building of the church went on all that summer and into September. The Synod of Utah at its last meeting the fall previous decided to hold its next annual meeting in Pocatello. So it was necessary to have the building completed by the time Synod was to meet. And it was done. The whole thing was completed by the last of September and Synod was to meet the first week in October. The work of procuring entertainment for the coming delegates fell mostly on my shoulders. There were few women to help and the officers of the congregation were busy men in business who could not give much time to aid in the preparation. Beside the entertainment there was also the arranging of the program which was no small matter as it took much correspondence. Above all that there had arrived in June of that year in our home a fine baby boy which had grown by this time into a lusty youngster of four or five months for whose care I was partly responsible. He was the pride and center of affection of the whole household which he has held all of these years.

Not much help did I get from my Sunday School superintendent who was also elder and clerk of the congregation and chairman of the building committee. Besides being a busy man of business he yet was unfriendly on account of the resubmission of the bids. About all he would consent to do was to promise to entertain a particular minister and his wife in his home. For the rest of the time he found fault with all we were doing in the way of preparation for Synod. In justice however it must be said that he didn't know all that had to be done in the way of preparation. I am sure that if I had consulted with him more and asked his advice that his attitude would have been very different. In the end he was very gracious; for when a very successful meeting of synod was brought to a close he said that its success was due to the preparation I had made for it and he didn't see how I had done it. What misunderstandings could be cleared up if we were led always by the Spirit of Christ.

An Ideal Executive

At that meeting was Dr. Wishard, ruddy of face, cheerful, helpful, ready to counsel, and influencing the whole synod by his quick intuition of what was needed to be done and said. He was one of the greatest of our home missionaries and a great Christian soul. He was always ready to plant an outpost on our far flung frontier and to raise Immanuel's banner in every out of the way place he could. He was a great executive with great evangelistic power. He laid the foundation of the temple of God on "the foundation of the apostles and prophets, Jesus Christ being the chief corner stone." There was no compromise with him. He resigned his position of synodical missionary at that meeting of synod and it was the last he ever attended. He had reached an age when he could no longer do the work as efficiently and promptly as he thought it should be done. Rev. Josiah McClain was elected to fill his place, a man well qualified and with whom I had fine fellowship in days to come. He was frequently in my home.

Dr. McClain told me a beautiful story of Dr. Wishard that shows his ardent and lovely spirit. When the First Presbyterian Church of Salt Lake City under the leadership of Dr. Paden had built their beautiful new house of worship the old building was left standing on its lot for sometime afterward. It had been the center of the historic missionary work of the Presbyterian denomination in Utah. The night before Dr. Wishard was to leave Utah to go to California to spend the rest of his days Dr. McClain was passing by the old church building when he thought he heard talking in the rear of it. Listening he was sure of it. Wondering who could be there at that time of night he slipped around to the back and there found Dr. Wishard upon his knees pleading with God for Utah and all the vast region that had been under his supervision. That tells the story of a great and successful missionary. Dr. McClain slipped away humbled yet greatly inspired.

A Distinguished Young Man

One of the distinguished men at that meeting of synod was John Willis Baer secretary of the United Society of Christian Endeavor and afterward to become a Moderator of the General Assembly. At that time he was as famous as any living young man of that day and indeed as famous as any. Through some hitch in our entertainment plans we were obliged to receive him and Mrs. Baer who was with him in our home. They were a delightful couple and made the best of everything. Particularly was Mrs. Baer delighted with the baby boy. They had no children of their own and she spent hours playing with the baby and taking great interest in his daily bath. She was a very gracious lady.

Mr. Baer afterward became president of Occidental College and a Moderator of the Presbyterian General Assembly and later president of a bank in Pasadena. He died several years ago at the age of seventy-one, one of the most useful and beloved men of his generation. How he could delight and thrill a convention of young people with his beautifully formed sentences his fine voice and graceful presence and great messages. Above all his great Christian character shone forth in all that he said and did. America never produced in one generation a greater trio of young leaders than Robert E. Speer, John R. Mott, and John Willis Baer. They were an inspiration to a countless number of young people and as they grew older to a multitude of men and women.

At the close of the morning service of the meeting of synod and just before the communion service we brought our baby boy forward to be baptized. We had asked Dr. Wishard to baptize him which he graciously consented to do. And lovingly and with great dignity he did it. We have always regretted that we did not have John Willis Baer assist Dr. Wishard as an elder and present at the service. He told us afterward that he wished heartily that he might but didn't like to suggest it. Being concerned about many things it slipped our minds. We felt like the man in the parable of the Scriptures who was given a prisoner to guard but let him escape. In his report to the king he said ''And while thy servant was busy here and there he was gone.''

After the meeting of synod when all the ministers and elders and mission teachers had gone back to their work and homes our own work went on slowly, ponderously, with the constant strain of the ever widening breach between myself and the elder who never wanted to be an elder and said he should not have been put in the position. In that he was right and honest. It was a continual source of sorrow to me. It was hindering both spiritual and visible growth. One year had gone by, a year of toil and worry. To be sure we had built a modest little church building sufficient for all present needs. We had just successfully entertained a large meeting of synod and there was much to encourage us. But we had incurred a debt of a thousand dollars in building and that was a heavy burden for a little home mission congregation to carry.

Here was a place where the then Board of Church Erection ought to have assumed more than a third of the whole cost. It was a pure mission enterprise just starting and should have been recognized as such and provided for as any other mission enterprise in Mormon country was provided for. True it was not a mission to Mormons but to just as hard to reach and irreligious Gentiles who cared not a whit whether the church lived or died. Though in the years following it did struggle out from under the burden of that debt and has today a fifty thousand dollar building in place of the old, what courage it would have given to the little congregation of those days and how much sooner it would have attained self support if the Board had assumed three fourths of the cost at least.

Had it not been for the hearty support of one man and his wife and the faithfulness of a few others we would have been utterly discouraged. That one man and his wife were Mr. and Mrs. E. C. White whose names I mention here because they have been the mainstay of the church for more than thirty years. We were given grace to hold on and slowly, very slowly the work grew into permanency. We gained one here and another there until we had quite a respectable little congregation. There were several things that held us back. First of all of course was my own inefficiency and lack of spiritual wisdom and power. Then the little church was always behind in meeting its part of the salary. That embarrassed us greatly. There was a fine new Congregational church building on the west side. It had a brilliant pastor who loved all sports and hunting especially. He was a good preacher and he and his family were good friends of myself and family. They had me baptize their last baby. Most of the Presbyterians who had been in the city for years were members of that church. Those who were newly arrived for the most part joined it attracted by the social and numerical advantages of a larger congregation. One could scarcely blame them. Then nearly all of the east side where our church was located was Mormon. There were about three thousand of them. Their influence and numbers made me feel as though I was dwelling among a foreign people who spoke an entirely different tongue than myself. All the Gentile churches felt the same way. While there was no open hostility, all felt that secretly the work of the Gentile churches was being greatly hindered by the subtle methods of the Mormon leaders and people.

Mormon Influence in Politics and Religion

To show the extent of the Mormon influence in politics and religion at that time the incident I am about to relate will show. What it may be after thirty or more years I do not know. One Fourth of July, I think it was the second we had spent in the city, a great celebration was planned. The speaking program was to be held in McNichols and Wrights Hall which was the largest auditorium in the city. The speaker of the day was the supreme judge of Idaho an elder in a church that I afterward served. When the audience was gathered together in the auditorium I sat among them with other gentile ministers scattered here and there. On the platform and towards the rear sat the speaker of the day who was a Presbyterian elder. On his right was the mayor of the city and chairman of the day who was superintendent of the Methodist Sunday School; next to him on the right was the president of the First National Bank who was superintendent of the Congregational Sunday School and a deacon; both of these were seeking nomination for governor by the next Republican State convention. Next to these and at their right was the judge of the District Court who wanted to be United States Federal Judge. He was superinendent of the Baptist Sunday

School and a deacon in the church. The speaker of the day was seeking the nomination for United States senator by the next Republican convention. All of these were strong and brilliant men and pillars in their respective churches.

To the left of the speaker on the platform was the bishop of the local Mormon church; to his left was the president of the Mormon stake and five of his counselors; then came the prosecuting attorney of the county a Mormon who read the Declaration of Independence. Not a single gentile minister was asked to sit on the platform or have any part in the proceedings though the mayor was chairman and a good Methodist. All of these men were out for the Mormon vote. I learned that politics and religion make strange alliances at times. I learned also that religious beliefs can be easily set aside by its most prominent representatives if it was thought that thereby there might be some personal advantage accruing to them.

How a Jury Was Selected

One other incident happened to me here that gives us a slant on another phase of Mormon influence in judicial affairs at the time, though it happens among gentiles as well. A drayman that had several times made deliveries to me of wood and coal was arrested and tried for the killing of an Indian from off the Shoshone reservation close by. One day I was going by the court house and knowing that the court was trying this very case I decided to go up to the court room and look on for awhile. I found a seat in the rear of the court room which was filled with spectators. The attorneys were just finishing the examination of the last man of the special venire that had been called to sit on the case. He was accepted but as yet there were only ten men accepted for jury service. And the venire was exhausted.

Then the judge, a Mormon, said to the sheriff, a jack Mormon, "Mr. Sheriff look around the court room and if you see anyone eligible for jury service call him." After a short time I felt the eyes of the sheriff fixed on me and I slid down in my seat to hide if possible. But to no avail. I heard him say "Your Honor, there is Mr. Hedges down there." I heard the judge say "Mr. Hedges, come up and be sworn." Feeling like a criminal myself I got up and went forward to the jury box where I was sworn to give correct answers to the questions asked me relative to my fitness to serve on the jury in this particular case.

Both the prosecuting attorney who was a Mormon and the attorney for the defense who was a Mormon sympathizer asked me the usual questions and both accepted me as a juror. I sat there as I thought a full fledged juror on a murder trial. The judge then declared a recess and ordered the court bailiff to take the jury out for an airing and the sheriff to go down town and subpoena anyone eligible for jury service.

In the course of half an hour or more the sheriff returned with several men whom he had picked up and the jury was taken back up to the court room and into the jury box. After their names were called the attorney for the defense got up and said, ''Your Honor, we would like to excuse Mr. Hedges from jury service on this case.'' Then the prosecuting attorney sprang to his feet and with great show of indignation said, ''Your Honor, we object. Mr. Hedges is the best qualified juror we have.'' For a few minutes they argued the matter back and forth when the judge said ''We'll take no chances on this case. I'll excuse the juror. Mr. Hedges, you may go.'' Jumping to my feet I hurried away from that court room as fast as I could go and never went back.

It was easy to see why I was not wanted. The defendant was a Mormon; the judge afterward supreme judge of Idaho was a Mormon; the prosecuting attorney was a Mormon and the attorney for the defense was a jack Mormon; all the jury that had been selected were Mormons and the two who were yet to be selected would be Mormon. At any rate the drayman got off scott free though he had shot the Indian in the back. At least that has always been the reason which to my mind was the reason I was not wanted. From every standpoint I was well qualified. But I was glad to escape.

Who Threw the Fatal Bomb?

There is another experience that I had that seems well worth telling. Those were the days of that terrible crime when Ex-Governor Steunenberg whom I personally knew was blown to pieces at the gate of his home in Caldwell by a bomb fastened there or thrown from without the darkness of the night. It made a tremendous sensation not only throughout the state but throughout the United States. The people of Idaho were determined to bring the murderer or murderers to justice. A great national detective agency was employed and in due time they arrested one Harry Orchard who on promise of life imprisonment only confessed to having thrown the bomb; that it was part of a great plot of the American Federation of Miners out of revenge for the activities of Ex-Governor Steunenberg in suppressing the historic miners strike in the famous Coeur d'Alene mining district in the early nineties.

There was no doubt of the great brutality exhibited in the suppression of that strike. Men were herded into strong stockades called ''bull pens'' like cattle and kept there unable to observe the common decencies of life for days. An old U. S. Army colonel who either was commander or one of the commanders of regular army troops sent in there to enforce martial law told me much of the cruelty used to suppress the strike. Governor Steunenberg had gotten great blame for this among the miners and threats had been made against his life.

Orchard in his confession laid the blame for the conspiracy to kill the ex-governor on three officials of the Colorado Federation of Miners, Haywood, Pettibone, and Moyer. He was only the tool by which it was accomplished. These men were particularly obnoxious to the mine owners by reason of their activities in the then almost constant warfare between the miners and mine owners over wages and hours of labor and housing and labor conditions generally. In this the miners had the sympathy of a large part of the public until this brutal murder was committed when opinion became divided. Many hardly knew where to stand.

These three men, Haywood, Pettibone, and Moyer, were surreptitiously seized by Colorado authorities hurried to the Idaho state line and turned over to Idaho officials. They were hurried on to Boise without due process of extradition measures such as is common when some one is wanted by another state for an alleged crime committed therein. This seemed an injustice to many and won back for them much sympathy which had been turned away. There was much satisfaction however over the arrests in the state as well as dissatisfaction. Good citizens were greatly divided in their opinions and it was a time when it was better to keep still if one had the sense and will to do it.

In due time the prisoners were brought to trial centering on Haywood as chief conspirator. It was one in which not only the state of Idaho was interested but the whole nation. The young and brilliant prosecuting attorney of the state, William E. Borah, was the prosecutor for the state. Arrayed against him on the other side was a brilliant and subtle Chicago lawyer whom the miners regarded as their chief legal spokesman in the United States. He was resourceful and forceful. His name was Clarence E. Darrow. The trial brought both men into national prominence. For a long time it dragged its course through the Idaho courts and it was a question as to what would be the outcome. Every line in the newspapers that had any reference to the case was breathlessly scanned. Pocatello was thrilled when it was proved that the material of the bomb had been stored in an old warehouse a few blocks from my home.

When the testimony was all in and the masterly speeches of the attorneys summing up the evidence for and against were all over the whole state waited in an agony of suspension the findings of the jury. After hours of deliberation they came back into the court room and at the request of the judge for their decision the foreman arose and said, "Not guilty, your Honor." As the morning papers told the story various were the comments. Some would hang the jury; some declared that judge and jury were bought. But the vast majority of the people felt that no other verdict could have been given.

A Labor Leader Comes to Town

The next morning wandering down town I saw a great crowd of people gathered on the platform of the depot of the Oregon Short Line. Happening to meet the pastor of the Baptist church down town also I proposed to him to walk over to the depot to see what was going on. We found there about a thousand employees of the railroad shops with their wives and children. There was the shop band also playing all the while. They had received word that Haywood was on the incoming passenger train from the west having left Boise the night before with his wife and children and mother. He was on his way back to Colorado. The shop men had come down to see him and to congratulate him on his having been set free. Not a single business man was there. Nor an official of the railroad. Not a single representative of any civic or industrial institution. Not a lawyer or a physician. Just us two ministers and curiosity had taken us there.

Soon the word was passed that the train was coming. All trains bound east and west stopped there for fifteen or twenty minutes to change engines and crews and the replenishing and cleaning of coaches. The band lined up along the platform and a committee from the labor unions stepped forward while the great crowd of men, women, and children, lined up behind them. All were anxious to see the now famous Haywood. When the train had pulled in and come to a full stop Haywood was seen seated at open window of one of the Pullman coaches, big, smiling, dominant, with his wife and little daughters and mother. Then he was suddenly pulled to his feet and lifted to the shoulders of the welcoming committee and carried out to the platform.

There they placed him on one of the depot trucks amidst the loud cheering and clamors of the crowd and the playing of the band. He made a short speech in which he congratulated labor on the great victory it had won in Boise and bade them stand pat on the demands that labor was then making of all capitalistic enterprises. He emphasized the duty of all laboring men to stand together in the one common purpose of seeing that labor secured all the rights to which it was entitled by the laws of God and man. I stood close by the truck and could have reached forth my hands at any moment and congratulated him. But as much as I sympathized with labor I was afraid lest I might be congratulating one deserving of punishment from which he had only escaped by cunning manipulation of evidence. But I am glad that I saw and heard him.

Politics and Government at Close Range

I had an interesting political experience here in Pocatello one of which I am quite proud in a way. It was interesting because it notes the beginning of the senatorial career of one of our most distinguished United States senators, William E. Borah. From the very moment of his arrival in the state as a young lawyer he captured the public fancy. In his prosecution of Haywood as attorney general of the state he won a nation wide reputation. The Republican party held its state convention in Pocatello the year after that trial. It is just thirty years ago as I write this story. Being a republican and being on good terms with many of the leading republicans of the state I was asked to sit in a caucus with state leaders the purpose of which was to choose a name to be presented to the convention for its indorsement as its nominee for United States senator. It was overwhelmingly voted to place Mr. Borah's name before the convention though it was hard to pin him down to any one thing. He turned several somersaults in the course of the discussion. As we were departing from the caucus I said to Congressman Burton L. French who with his wife was a good friend of myself and family. "Burton, You'll never be able to pin Borah down to any thing definite. He will always be a free lance." And that prophesy has been fulfilled in the thirty years of his brilliant career in the senate more than fulfilled. I have always been glad that I was at that caucus and jokingly have said that I helped to make him senator. Always has he stood at the very front of our great statesmen. Always has he stood for the highest and best in citizenship and statesmanship. But he has always been Borah fighting his own battles in his own way, and standing for his own policies loyal to his party if its policies coincided with his own but loyal to himself first.

Soon after the aquittal of Haywood President Theodore Roosevelt made some very offensive remarks about the lawlessness of the state and sent his secretary of state, William H. Taft, to Idaho to make a couple of speeches on lawlessness. It was an affront to the good citizens of the state who were for the most part intelligent and law abiding. No western state had a finer type of citizenship in general. The state as a whole had been anxious to make an example of these men if they were guilty. But as the evidence was brought out from day to day many began to think that it was not sufficient to connect them with the crime. Most people believed that the jury had honestly done its duty and had not been tampered with in any way. So they considered President Roosevelt's inconsiderate remarks and his inconsiderate act in sending Mr. Taft to the state to talk on lawlessness as an affront to themselves.

At any rate Secretary Taft came and made his two speeches in the state one at Pocatello and the other at Boise. I heard him at Pocatello where he was under the escort of Governor Gooding. He changed no one's opinion, restored no order to the state, added nothing to good citizenship, and made no friends for the administration. Possibly he went back to Washington with feeling of satisfaction with a duty well performed. But Mr. Roosevelt was never so popular in Idaho after that. It was felt that he was too ready with the "Big Stick"; too ready to shout "Ananias" when there was no occasion. Many felt like saying "Upon what meat hath this our Caesar fed that he has grown so great."

A humiliating experience in connection with my church work came to me that I am going to tell as showing how with the best of intentions we may do things that give evil minded men occasion to speak ill of us and temporarily at least hurt us in the eyes of others. During the last year I was there we had a new member of the session a brilliant young civil engineer who was also Division Engineer of the Short Line. He was well spoken of and worthy. He was a close social friend of the other elder who had been Sunday School superintendent, clerk of the session, and treasurer of the church. He had resigned all of these offices and had quit coming to church, and more and more outspoken in his enmity to me and the church. Because there was no one who could be immediately put in as treasurer I took charge of collections, paid janitor, light bills, and other expenditures until we could find a treasurer.

Both of these men were inclined to be snobbish belonging to the same social group that was classed as the leading social group of the city. They were anxious only that we receive into our little group only those of like social standing. There was a poor family whom I had called on and induced to come to church and Sunday School. There was a father and mother and three children. One Sunday evening they were all present at the service. I preached an evanglistic sermon that night and then gave an invitation and opportunity for any one to confess Jesus Christ. To my surprise and delight this whole family came forward desiring to be received into the church. I called the young engineer who was my only acting elder to come forward and after prayer we examined them one by one and received all of them into the Church. I saw that the young elder and engineer was not very enthusiastic and at the close of the service he came to me and said "Why do you receive such people into the church. They are of no advantage to us." I looked at him in amazement and could find no words to express my feelings. My heart was filled with sorrow and indignation.

Should a Minister Handle Church Funds?

What was my surprise one day to get a peremptory note from him demanding an accounting of the collections of which I had taken charge until a new treasurer could be found to take the place of the first elder who had been treasurer and who had ceased to act as such. He was induced to do this by this former treasurer and elder. The latter had called on me one morning to turn them over to him apparently thinking he could lay down an office at any time and resume functioning when he pleased. However I was not loathe for him to resume the duty if he would, but told him I had used them in paying the current expenses and some of my own money as well. He went away quite angry and stirred up the young engineer to demand an accounting evidently sowing the suspicion in the other's mind that I was applying these collections on my own personal obligations. I was to blame in not having called a congregational meeting immediately on his ceasing to function as treasurer and elect a new one. But material was scarce and no one wanted the office. So I made the great mistake of assuming the responsibility until we could find another.

A minister should never put himself in the way of suspicion by handling any part of the church's finances or acting as a receiving agency for various offerings. While in his own mind it might be inconceivable that he would ever use them for his own ends yet it is not inconceivable to other minds whether they be evil or not. Such was the case here. It didn't take long to clear myself of the charge and to show that the church was indebted to me not only for salary but for sums paid out from my own pocket for incidental expenses over and above the amount of the collections. Ever after that experience I have been careful not to handle church funds for any purpose except where it was absolutely necessary and then I kept strict account.

Our oldest daughter having developed a serious form of nervous trouble our physician told us that the altitude of Pocatello was much too high for her and we must go to a lower altitude if we wanted her to recover. The altitude of Pocatello was just a mile high and she needed almost sea level. This was the third year in this place. My wife and the children went north to spend the summer with her mother and father and brother in Kendrick while I stayed to finish out the year in Pocatello. Nothing of great importance happened that summer. I left October First after three years of as varied an experience in missionary work as one could wish or have. I was far from being satisfied. I left behind a little church not yet fully organized and a thousand dollar debt on the building. We had reduced this a little but not to any great extent. I was not sure that it would live or die and I was very anxious concerning it. Others, however, that came after me pushed the little church forward until it has become one of the strong churches of Idaho. "Paul may plant and Apollos may water but God giveth the increase."

How Irrigation Changed Yakima Valley

It was a new and entirely different experience to which I went when I went back to the Synod of Washington to become one of the pastors of the Federated Church of Sunnyside in the Yakima valley of central Washington. Here was a valley that had lain sun scorched and barren for centuries. In the spring of the year it was swept by dust storms which the winds blew before them in clouds and piled the dust up like snowdrifts around the sagebrush the only shrub that grew thereon. Jack rabbits were the only living things that could exist save rattlesnakes and lizards. Here the government was trying out its first major experiment in irrigation. Some ten years before it had constructed a great canal taking the water out of the Yakima river and extending the canal for twenty-five miles down the valley along its eastern edge and watering a strip of country below it from five to ten miles wide for the whole distance. The soil was wonderfully fertile being the loose silt of an old lake belt but it took much work to dig out the sage brush and level it up for irrigation. They called it the Sunnyside Project.

Here when I came were orchards and alfalfa fields and gardens that looked luxurious to me after the sage covered plains of southern Idaho. Here were the cozy homes of many substantial farmers and orchardists and gardeners living on tracts of from five to twenty and forty acres or more and drawing water for the irrigation of them from the great Sunnyside canal. When I first came there the whole irrigated section was disfigured here and there by acres of white and black alkali soil that once were green alfalfa fields and orchards. The ever rising water table from the constant irrigation brought the water finally to the surface in many places. Being saturated with the alkalies through which it passed and which it dissolved on its way upward to the surface it killed alfalfa and orchards and all kinds of other products. In other spots there were great swamps formed by the draining of the alkali water into large areas of depression in the valley floor. Finally the government while we were there put in a great drainage canal stretching clear across the valley and emptying into the Yakima river. This in time restored most of the lands that had gone to alkali.

There was a large population in the valley with a few centers in which lived the business and professional part of the population with schools and churches that were within easy reach of people living on their little ranches and orchard tracts. For the most part it was a church going population. The first Sunday morning I was there I was astonished at the great number of carriages and buggies and saddle ponies that were gathered around the Federated church building. It was before the days of the automobile. I asked some one if there was anything unusual going on at the church that day. He smiled and said that there were not as many as usual. Sunnyside was the chief town of that part of the valley with a population of about twelve hundred and a surrounding population of from three to four thousand people. I was astonished at the congregation that morning.

An Early Experiment in Church Federation

Here was being tried out the first great experiment in church federation in the United States. Or rather it had already been tried for about five years and this was the continuation of it. A colony of the Progessive Branch of the Church of the Brethren or Dunkars as they were commonly called had been the first to settle in this valley. They had bought much acreage from the government and established the town of Sunnyside and expected to settle it up with people of the Church of the Brethren of both branches. A few Methodists, Presbyterians, Baptists, Congregationalists Christians, and others had come in also at the opening of the Project. They all had organizations except the Presbyterians because of comity agreement with the Congregationalists. No one denomination was yet strong enough to maintain regular services. Nor were any of them able to build a building.

Rev. Stephen H. Harrison a minister of the Progressive Brethren and founder of the community, an able and prosperous man and liberal minded toward other communions, conceived the idea of a Federated Church in which all the organized religious bodies of the community should be constituent parts and should agree to enter it for five years. They were to pool their resources and erect a church building to seat a thousand people with prayer and young peoples' rooms. Each denomination in the Federation was to maintain its own organization pay its own pastor and use the building in proportion to its funds invested. In all other respects they were to be one, having one Sunday School, one prayermeeting and young people's society which was to be an Endeavor Society and an annual congregational meeting every year.

Into this Federation entered the Progressive Brethren, Methodists, Baptists, Congregationalists, and Christians. The Presbyterians were invited to organize and enter the Federation. This they did with the cordial consent of the Congregationalists. For five years it existed in this form with the greatest harmony prevailing between its various and radically different communions. The pastor of each group took his turn in preaching according to the pro rata contribution of that group to the church building fund. The Sundays they were not on duty here they were off to other points of the valley. In the course of time five other Presbyterian churches were organized the most of them by the pastor preceding me, the Rev. Rollin Blackman. The most of them are vigorous churches today.

When I arrived on the scene the old Federation had broken up in the preceding spring. There was general regret and weeping on the part of the members of each denomination. They had gotten along so finely together and had so greatly enjoyed their Christian fellowship and formed such intimate relationships that it was like the break up of a home. But the denominational zeal of the larger group, the Methodists, and the restlessness of such communions as the Baptist and Christian because they could not preach their particular views of Baptism, led these three groups to withdraw at the close of the five year agreement. Each group withdrawing sold its interest in the Federated building and built buildings of their own. The three remaining bodies, the Progressive Brethren, Congregationalists, and Presbyterians formed a new federation to last for three years and bought the interests of the three that had withdrawn in the old church building. The new Federation continued the policy of the former as regards services Sunday School, prayermeeting, and young peoples' societies. Each body had its own pastor who preached every third Sunday.

Irregular Financial Payments

It was as pastor of the Presbyterian group that I appeared on the scene. I was greatly delighted with the congregation that first day. It looked very large to me in comparison to the meager few of the field from which I had just come. Besides they seemed so serious and churchly minded that I felt as though my portion had indeed fallen in truly pleasant places. I was sure I was going to have a beautiful and glorious experience. Experience I had indeed but I wouldn't call it wonderful and glorious except by way of discipline at the hands of the Father. As I look back on my life there I can see how if my own attitude, spirit, and inefficiency had been different I might have had what the flesh considers a glorious experience all along the line. Also if the field that I served had always done its duty particularly in its financial support I might have had another glorious experience. Indeed the hardest thing about work on the home mission field was the irregularity with which that part of our salary promised by the field was paid. It never was fully paid. Hundreds of dollars are still due us out of all those years of the past. There was great comfort in the more or less small payments of the Board that reached us every month with great promptness. We knew to a cent that we should receive it and were very grateful to the great faithful Board that in times of prosperity and times of depression always stood by. But the work itself was our great remuneration. "I have meat to eat that ye know not of."

My salary on this field was one thousand dollars and no manse. I had three fields to serve the first two years which compelled me to keep a horse and buggy for which I received no extra allowance. I preached in Sunnyside every third Sunday. The other Sundays I preached in the morning at Grandview a newly opened orchard tract and in the evening at Mabton on the other side of the Yakima river which was irrigated by water siphoned under the river from the Sunnyside canal. It meant a drive of thirty three miles going and coming, attending four services, and getting home at midnight. The winters were cold and the summers were hot for driving in an open buggy. In summer the roads were dusty and full of dust holes and in winter were frozen ruts. I did this for three years until Grandview developed so much as to demand the services of a minister the entire time. And thereby hangs an interesting story of what the consecration of one man can accomplish when devoted to the service of God.

Bob Maynes was a miner in Roslyn in that state. In a revival meeting in our church there he was converted and he and his wife united with the church. When the government began to build the Sunnyside canal Bob went down into the sagebrush of the lower valley and took up a quarter section of land. It was about eight miles below the site of the future town of Sunnyside. In order to make a living for his family he would ride horseback across the sagebrush prairie and work on the extending canal and ride back at night. When the town of Sunnyside was established and the Federated church was organized he and his wife put in their membership with the Presbyterian portion of it. It wasn't long before the canal was extended far enough that he could put his place under irrigation. He had cleared and leveled about eighty acres of his quarter section and in a short time it was all one green alfalfa field with his home in about the center of it surrounded with trees which he set out as soon as he could get the water.

Every Sunday morning he loaded his family into an old fashioned dead ax wagon and drove across the eight miles of sagebrush over a rough road full of dust holes in the summer and ruts in the winter to Sunnyside to the Federated church. As time went on he had a more comfortable hack or spring wagon. When he was telling me about it one day he said "You know I was only a nominal Christian then. I thought it was my duty to take my family to church somewhere. The big Federated church took my fancy and relieved me of taking any responsibility. There was a little Presbyterian church and Sunday School on the banks of the Yakima three or four miles below me and my conscience often troubled me about that little church and Sunday School. Many times it was laid on me to take my family out of the big Federated church and join this other one. But my pride and indolence wouldn't let me."

Accident in a Well

The Lord has to discipline his people pretty hard sometimes before they are ready to do what he wants them to do. It was true of Bob Maynes. He had a neighbor just across the road from him who wanted a well dug. At that time wells were dug by hand and Maynes being an old miner was asked by his neighbor to help dig the well. He consented to do so and for several days the digging went on apace. When it had reached a depth of sixty feet and still no water one day at noon the owner who was at the windlass above called down to him and said "Bob, it is dinner time. Get into the bucket and I will haul you up." When the bucket reached the top and just as he was about to step out on the curb the bucket in some way was upturned and Bob was thrown out and headed for the bottom. He told me that as he started to fall that sixty feet he lifted up his voice and prayed "O Lord, if you will save my life to my wife and children I will do what you want me to do."

They went down after poor Bob. They found him alive but with a terribly injured and broken hip. They brought him up and carried him home where he lay for weeks. He finally recovered sufficiently to go about his work as formerly. But like Jacob he went halting on that thigh till the day of his death which it caused eventually. He knew now what he ought to do, what the Lord wanted him to do. He took his membership and family out of the Federated church in Sunnyside and went to the little struggling Presbyterian church and Sunday School on the banks of Yakima. Here they made him superintendent of the Sunday School and it wasn't long before he had the church building overflowing with people attending the Sunday School. Then they built a new schoolhouse of two rooms on his own farm for which he gave ground. He organized a Sunday School there and in a short while he had that schoolhouse filled with people. About the same time the Grandview Orchard Tract Company laid out the beautiful Grandview Orchard Tracts and established the town of Grandview some two or three miles distant from his home.

The company built a large two story frame school building and thither Bob Maynes removed the Sunday School by the river and the Sunday School from the school house on his own place to the new schoolhouse in Grandview. Here is where I first met him. I went out there to preach the second Sunday I was in the valley. I saw a great crowd of buggies and carriages and saddle horses hitched all around the building. As at Sunnyside the previous Sunday I was astonished and inquired if there was anything unusual going on and was told that it was the usual thing. When I went in and met the fairhaired and energetic little man limping from room to room and was greeted with a wonderful smile, I understood.

For the three years I served that field with Sunnyside and Mabton and the little church down on the river Bob Maynes kept me on the road much of the time. He would call me on the telephone and say "There's a new family just moved into the community. I wish you would drive down and see them." Or "Sadie Smith wants to be baptized next Sunday, You ought to see her." Or "Mr. Patton is very sick. He would like to see you." There were many other such requests coming constantly over the phone. Finally we moved the little old church building from the river across four miles of sagebrush and through orchard tracts to Grandview. We built an addition to it for Sunday

School purposes that could be thrown into the main auditorium altogether accommodating about five hundred people. We secured a young man for pastor who came to us from the Southern Methodist Church. He was a graduate of Emory College who had taken a special course in speaking. He was very capable and very fine. It wasn't long before he and Bob Maynes had that whole building full to overflowing. And the Lord had to let a man fall sixty feet into a well before he could see what he must do.

One day he came riding up to my home in Sunnyside just a short while before he died somewhere about noon. We put his horse in the stable as he was going to be with us for dinner. We went into the living room and sat down and talked about various things though I could see that he had something on his mind of which he wanted to speak. Suddenly he said to me, "Do you know that I have never been baptized." "Will you baptize me?" Very much astonished I said "Why, Mr. Maynes, how is that? Were you not baptized when you united with the church in Roslyn?" He said "No, I was not. I suppose the minister thought that I had been baptized in infancy and I didn't realize the importance of it then. But I feel that I can not go on urging young people to make a confession of their faith and be baptized when I have not been baptized myself. And besides I feel that in all good conscience I should be baptized." "Well," I said, "there is no man I would rather baptize than you." And taking some water we went up into my study and there kneeling on my study floor I baptized him. It was an answer of a good conscience to God. A few months afterward he died. But his work still goes on.

Problems of Church Union

After Grandview had the whole time of a minister and a minister of its own I took on Liberty where was a small Federated church of Methodists and Presbyterians. I served the Presbyterian group which though the smallest was the most influential. At Sunnyside my difficulties were chiefly ecclesiastical. There was a small but influential group in our church who were always holding out for the abandonment of our church and its union with the Congregationalists. They were mostly those who had once been Congregationalists and through marriage had become identified with us. When I first came to Sunnyside and saw the situation and realized the struggle that both would have alone I proposed the same thing at a meeting of the session. My principal reason however was respect for the old comity agreement between the two denominations which had been in effect for a hundred years. But when I broached it to the session one of the elders told me to forget it for the Congregationalist higher ups had cordially consented to our organization at the time the federation of churches was formed in Sunnyside. He afterward became one of the strongest advocates of the union and abandonment of our work.

This refusal to abandon our work and unite with them became more and more a source of irritation between the two bodies though more or less kept hidden. It was also a source of irritation in our own group as there were a few who desired the thing very much. In the Federation as it now existed those in our body who desired the union were throwing their influence to the pastor of the Congregationalist church and snubbing me. This naturally brought about a more or less irritation between us though both of us tried not to show it. He was a fine, intelligent, well educated, and well traveled, and agreeable little man whom people in general liked and whose preaching they enjoyed better than my own. But he was oversensitive and a bit inclined to think we were trying to put something over on him, also a bit conceited. I am inclined to think he would say the same things of me. For he was a courteous Christian gentleman.

As the months went on and the time drew near for the ending of our three years agreement in Federation the uncertainty and feeling grew apace. Should we all withdraw and go our separate ways or should we federate again or should the two of us unite. Agitation within our own group by the small and influential party that wanted union grew stronger. The majority of the Presbyterians neither wanted union or federation. Down in my own heart I was for it if it could be worked out satisfactorily for the good of the kingdom of God. I felt out one of the leading members of the Congregationalist church one day who was also a deacon. I made the suggestion to him that I would resign as pastor of the Presbyterian church if the pastor of his own church would resign also. This would get us both out of the way and enable the two churches to get together on some kind of a Christian basis that would not involve the retention of either pastor. Neither one of us would be wholly acceptable to both bodies.

But my proposition was rejected with scorn by the good deacon who said "Who wants our pastor to resign?" I saw at once that he thought that the small influential group in the Presbyterian church would force the union anyhow and so neither he nor his group were disposed to make any concessions. My conscience and judgment being clear that there was no other way out I called a congregational meeting in order to lay before them the matter of withdrawing from the Federation at the end of the three years, of which only a few months yet remained, and of going by ourselves. The congregational meeting was well attended by a large representation of the whole church. Only one of the small influential group favoring union was absent, a merchant and his family. When the vote was taken after a long and for the most part courteous and Christian discussion it was found to be overwhelmingly in favor of withdrawal and going by ourselves. To the credit of those who were in favor of union be it said that they for most part acquiesced to the will of the majority and in fact I think they were glad. The one of them who was absent from the meeting, the merchant of whom I have spoken met me on the street the next morning and in a loud bellowing voice shouted, "You can have no more credit from me, Sir."

Values and Weaknesses in Federation

At my next preaching service I announced that the Presbyterians had decided to withdraw and go by themselves. The Progressive Brethren also announced their intention to withdraw and offered to buy the interests of the Presbyterians and Congregationalists in the old church building. This they did and made some greatly needed improvements to the building and installed a pipe organ. The Presbyterians and Congregationalists continued to worship together in the Baraca building a building erected by all of the Baraca classes of the community for recreational and interclass doings. We continued to worship together until our separate buildings were ready for occupancy. Ours was a beautiful and commodious frame building and theirs was a substantial and good looking and well arranged cement block structure. In the years since both have developed into strong churches.

The Federation was dissolved in June and we dedicated our church building the following June. It took almost a year to arrange for and build it. Without question it was the most beautiful auditorium in the community at the time. And so ended a church federation that had existed in various forms for eight years. It was the first experiment in church federation that had ever been tried in this country, at least of any sizability, and attracted much attention. In many ways it was a great success. It proved that Christians of different groups could work and worship together harmoniously; that all twice born men and women speak the same language; that a united body of Christian believers in a community can wholly effect and secure moral and spiritual conditions in which to rear a family; that living together and working together as one family its members lose that scorn of one another so frequently seen in separated bodies.

On the other hand there was the necessity of giving up some vital preaching along doctrinal lines or what some consider as vital such as baptism upheld by all Baptist and Disciple groups or Calvinistic and Arminian views of predestination and free will as held by the Presbyterians and Methodists lest offense be given to the others. There was a weakness in missionary instruction and giving. We could not make our appeals for our separate missionary enterprises lest we be accused of taking an unfair advantage bringing them before the federated congregation. To the ministers who served the united congregations if there were more than one the situation was intolerable try as hard as one might to feel otherwise. The pastor who has had the love and confidence of one congregation finds it a little difficult to share it with another. Other federations were tried and are being tried in various parts of the country and some of them are quite satisfactory but I think the majority are not. They cannot be under the circumstances but sometimes they are far better than two or three struggling denominational bodies.

Sunnyside as a community was unique from its very beginning as an experiment in irrigation and also as a moral and religious experiment. Here its founders hoped to build up a segment of the kingdom of God on earth. Only Christian men and women were urged to come there. No saloon was allowed; private pool rooms were rigidly excluded; gambling of any kind was visited with chastisement; the dance had no favor; and card playing was considered a great disgrace. They who had the hardihood to try such things often found themselves excluded from the society of their neighbors. It was given the title of "The Holy City" by the profane dwellers of Sodom. Without doubt few communities could surpass it in intelligence and the love of good schools, lyceum courses, and the like. To offset the private pool rooms the commercial club fitted up a fine suite of rooms with billiard tables and reading room and gymnasium with comfortable rockers and chairs for the use of the young men of the community. No gambling of any kind was permitted and it was under rigid supervision. There being no tang to it the young men carefully avoided it. This was twenty five years ago. What changes have been made I do not know.

Index

The James A. Hedges PIONEER PREACHER IN IDAHO *was printed in the workshop of Glen Adams, which is located in the sleepy country village of Fairfield, Washington. This southern Spokane County farming area is one township removed from the Idaho line. The pages were faithfully photographed from the old periodical printing so the book is essentially a facsimile of earlier work except that subheads were changed to a more suitable typeface, fresh page numbers were added, title page and colophon. The added typesetting was done by Glen Adams using a Compugraphic 48 computer photosetter. The face for the photoset material is Baskerville in twelve point size. Page numbers are in Baskerville Bold. The title page is hand set Bembo and Bembo Titling and was printed by Glen Adams using a 14½ x 22 open platen press. The offset text was printed by Robert LaTendresse using a 770CD Hamada offset press. Camera-darkroom work was by Evelyn Foote Clausen. Indexing is by Edward J. Kowrach, who also assisted with the assembly of the book. The introduction to the book was written by E. Paul Hovey of Portland, Oregon, to whom I give my thanks. Binding is by William Bosch of Oakesdale, Washington. Paper stock is sixty pound Simpson Opaque. This was a fun project. We had no special difficulty with the work.*

Elk River
NORTH FORK
Headquarters
Bruces Eddy Damsite
Orofino
To Lewiston
Pierce
Clearwater
Greer
Weippe
River
Kamiah
Nez Perce
Cottonwood
Kooskia
Grangeville
S. FORK